SIMPLE DISHES THAT LOOK AFTER THEMSELVES

FROM THE OVEN TO THE TABLE

DIANA HENRY

MITCHELL BEAZLEY

CONTENTS

Closing the oven door and swinging a tea towel over my shoulder is one of the most satisfying movements I make in the kitchen. I love the alchemy that takes place behind that door. It's astonishing how heat, on its own – without you directing it or supervising it very much – can turn simple ingredients into a meal.

Because I love cooking, I'm happy to make complicated food; I know that some dishes can only be achieved by browning the constituent elements and slowly building layers of flavour. There will never come a time when I don't want to cook and eat *boeuf bourgignon*, a dish that needs this kind of attention. But I can't cook food like this from Monday to Thursday, I just don't have the time. If you're a bung-it-in-the-oven kind of cook, whether by necessity or desire, then this book is for you.

The dish that introduced me to this laidback oven-loving approach was an Antonio Carluccio recipe for chicken thighs cooked with little potatoes, red onion wedges, garlic, rosemary and olive oil. When I discovered it – it's in his book *An Invitation to Italian Cooking* – I silently mouthed the word 'genius' and knew that I had stumbled across something life-changing. For that dish, you don't brown anything, you just put the ingredients in a roasting tin, season them, put them in the oven and wait for 45 minutes. Then you eat. It's still the meal I have cooked more than any other over the last 20 years.

In that time, I've built up a repertoire of dishes on this theme, some with a layer of stock poured underneath the meat; as the dish cooks the top becomes golden and a sauce develops below. I worked out how to apply this approach to rice instead of potatoes, the stock reducing and being absorbed as the grains cook to tenderness. I roast foods that are more usually done in a pan on the hob – sausages, broccoli and salmon fillets – just because I think it's easier. It is literally 'hands off' cooking.

Why is it important, when I know that cooking does take effort, to offer you dishes that, while requiring attention, are relatively easy to achieve? Because I believe that the table is important. I wouldn't have managed to feed my children well and share food with friends (on a Wednesday as well as on a Saturday night) without finding simple ways to do things. The dishes that follow – from homely sausages baked with tomatoes, potatoes and pecorino cheese to a celebratory dish of sea bass with a Middle Eastern stuffing – have helped.

Because I roast and bake so much, I've amassed loads of roasting tins, baking sheets, gratin dishes and two broad shallow casseroles (though, truthfully, you only need one).

I'm not the only person who likes this kind of cooking. There are scores of American books devoted to 'sheet pan cooking'. We're not so familiar with sheet pans in the UK, but they're a great invention: heavy-gauge baking sheets with a lip around them. If you have sheet pans, you can use them instead of roasting tins or trays for many of the dishes in this book.

You don't need lots of new equipment to cook the food that follows, but it's a good idea to read the section on kit.

In the UK, people have started to call these dishes – cooked in roasting tins or oven trays – 'tray bakes', a term I just can't use, because, when I was growing up, tray bakes were exclusively sweet. Millionaire's shortbread, lemon bars, those squares made with cornflakes and golden syrup… these were 'tray bakes', so you won't find the term used here.

Many of the recipes that follow are for one-pot meals, but not all of them. When I have been able to incorporate a starch, I have. With some, I just wanted to give you a basic roast. With others, I felt that an accompanying grain, bread or salad was what you needed. There are no pasta dishes baked from raw in a roasting tin, as I hate the texture that produces. Pasta – like bulgur wheat – is actually easier to make on the hob, anyway.

So that you don't have to consult other books when cooking out of this one, I've included a page on how to cook various grains, and two pages on how to cook potatoes and sweet potatoes in the oven in lots of different ways alongside whatever else you are roasting.

Where the dishes are one-pot, they vary in terms of effort. The most basic really do just require you to chuck ingredients in a pan, season them and roast them. At the other end of the scale – as in a smoked fish, tomato and potato gratin, for example – you have to slice potatoes thinly and heat cream and milk before pouring it into the gratin dish. Some recipes are for fairly plain roasts that are made more special by a relish or a salsa on the side. You can choose whether to make the relish or not (I have suggested simpler accompaniments that you can buy), and there are also two pages of relish recipes that only require you to mix or chop, so you can ring the changes.

To cook this way – using very simple methods – you do need a well-stocked cupboard. You're not doing much to the food you're cooking, so you need big flavours. There are ingredients – pomegranate molasses, miso, preserved lemons – that you need to get. A lot of unusual foods that weren't available even five years ago are now sold in supermarkets, but if you don't have a good one near you, everything can be ordered online. I grew up in a small town where many things were impossible to buy. I wish we'd had the access to ingredients we do now. Delivery costs are an issue, but put together a list of things you need and then order them together, so you only have one delivery fee.

You don't just roast in the oven, of course, you also pot-roast, bake and do what Americans call 'wet roast' and I've written more about these later in the book. (There's not much science, just enough to help.) I do love what the application of dry heat – proper roasting – does to food, though, the way it caramelizes the surface of meat and the edges of vegetables. This heat can even help a batch of under-ripe and woolly apricots: roasted with a light dusting of sugar, the heat intensifies everything that is hidden when they're raw, it finds their sweetness, chars spots on their flesh, makes them tender and mouth-puckeringly tart.

Ovens used to have more of a physical presence in the home. Roasting and baking was done on an open hearth, not in a closed box with a glass front. Snowed in one year in Friuli in Northern Italy, I discovered the *fogolar*, a raised cooking area in the middle of the kitchen or living room with a chimney above it. Everyone gathered round this to get warm while the snow kept us prisoner, but it also provided many of our meals. It's convenient to have the oven against the wall in modern kitchens, tucked away, closed off, slick with dials. But it doesn't give it the status it deserves. In my mind, and in my cooking, the oven is central.

COOKING KIT

Do you need any fancy bits of equipment to cook from this book? Nope. But a few roasting tins are, obviously, a must-have (that way you can roast more than one dish in the oven at the same time). Some of mine have been on the go for thirty years, and the more bashed and worn they become, the more I love them. You need a heavier gauge tin that you can use on the hob as well as in the oven (essential for reducing cooking juices), and a few lighter ones. Lighter weight tins are often not suitable for using over direct heat, though, as they buckle, so choose the roasting tin according to what you're going to do with it. A mixture of sizes is important. You'll notice that I often suggest the components of a dish 'lie snugly' together. That's because if there's a lot of room around food that's roasting, the juices will evaporate and can, if they're in the oven long enough, burn. In lots of the recipes, the ingredients have to lie in a single layer (because if they lie on top of each other they sweat or steam rather than browning), so you need a very large roasting tin – or two medium-sized tins – that will hold everything. Roasting and baking are simple, but you have to follow the instructions.

I hate being didactic – many recipes are just blueprints on which you can put your own stamp – but the food won't turn out well if you don't pay attention to the size of the dish, if one is specified. This is especially the case if the recipe contains stock or cream; it has been tested so that a specific quantity of liquid will reduce to the right amount in the time and at the temperature given. The size of the cooking vessel will affect this.

I also have a few baking trays (and you will see items called 'oven trays'). These have lips around them of varying depths, but always shallower than the sides of roasting tins. They're really useful and usually lighter than roasting tins.

The other essential is a shallow casserole. Many of the recipes in the book have been tested and cooked in the dishes I use most often, a couple of 30cm (12in) shallow casseroles. I have one from Netherton Foundry (a small British company based in Shropshire) that is made of spun iron and is 5cm (2in) deep. The other is cast iron, made by Chasseur and is 6.5cm (2½in) deep. You can serve out of them as well as cook in them (though I don't object to serving out of a roasting tin; there's one on my table right now). Denby and Le Creuset also make cast iron versions in the correct size, but they're expensive (Le Creuset is now pretty much unaffordable). There are cheaper options, though. Paella pans – make sure to get one that, again, is 30cm (12in) across – can be bought for less than a tenner, though of course you have to be sure that the quality is good. Make sure, too, that the pan doesn't have plastic-covered handles, as they can't go in the oven. A ceramic pudding dish with a capacity of two litres (three and a half pints) is useful for the baked puddings that are in the 'Something Sweet' chapter.

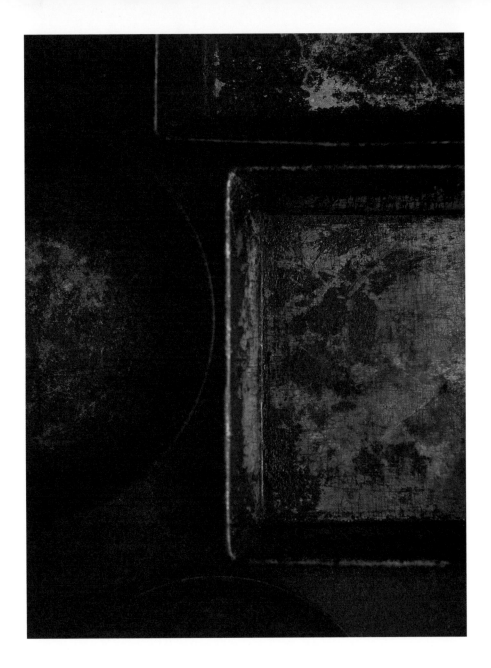

Some gratin dishes – the ones used in the book are made of enamel or cast iron and have capacities of one and two litres (one and three-quarters and three and a half pints) – are important too, as well as a frying pan that can be used on the hob and in the oven (so it shouldn't have a plastic or a wooden handle, or a non-stick coating).

I'm not keen on gadgets, but I do have good knives, a zester, a citrus juicer, a mandolin for slicing potatoes finely (you need this for only one dish in this book, though a good sharp knife will also do the job, albeit more slowly) and a mortar and pestle. A mortar and pestle, though old-fashioned, is sometimes better than a food processor, especially for bashing toasted spices and for making chunky relishes.

A CUPBOARD TO LOVE

Gone are the days when a home had a larder or pantry, a huge storage space packed with myriad possibilities to help you make dinner: tins and jars of preserved goods, spices, all manner of grains and pulses. Now we mostly have built-in cupboards, often so deep that you give up trying to find the ingredient you know is in there.

Because I grew up in a small town where it was impossible to find unusual ingredients, one of my greatest pleasures is stocking up with interesting bits and pieces, and I love cooking with them. Packets and jars of foods used in Japan or Korea or Sicily bring new experiences as well as dinner.

When you cook using simple methods – such as roasting – the interest often comes from the ingredients you add to a pan of chicken thighs or salmon fillets. Here, then, are the things it would be useful to have to hand when you're cooking from this book. You don't need to have them all at the same time, but if you're putting a selection together – or want to make an online order – bear these in mind. (And, for stockists, *see* page 234.)

OILS AND VINEGARS Extra virgin olive oil, groundnut oil, sesame oil, cider vinegar, white balsamic vinegar, sherry vinegar, rice vinegar

TINS AND JARS Anchovies, unsweetened coconut milk and coconut cream, canned tomatoes, black and green olives, preserved lemons, pickled chillies, capers, gherkins, stem ginger

CONDIMENTS, PASTES AND SAUCES White and red miso paste, harissa, pomegranate molasses, light and dark soy sauces, chilli sauce (such as sriracha), Thai fish sauce, tahini, Dijon mustard, chipotle paste, tamarind paste, *gochujang* hot pepper paste, mayonnaise, tomato purée, *kecap manis* (Indonesian soy sauce)

SPICES Cumin and coriander (both ground and seeds), chilli flakes, paprika and smoked paprika, saffron, cardamom, turmeric, fennel seeds, cinnamon (ground and sticks), bay leaves, cayenne pepper, black peppercorns, caraway, ginger, nutmeg, sea salt flakes

GRAINS AND PULSES Basmati rice, Spanish paella rice, short-grain pudding rice, Puy lentils, freekeh, couscous, bulgur wheat, barley, tins of white beans (cannellini and haricot) and black beans, dried haricot and cannellini beans, tinned chickpeas, pouches of ready-cooked lentils and grains (such as freekeh, barley and mixed grains)

NUTS, SEEDS AND DRIED FRUITS I tend to buy nuts as I need them because some – walnuts, for instance – turn rancid quite quickly, but these are what I always have in my kitchen: flaked almonds, blanched almonds, ground almonds, blanched hazelnuts, shelled unsalted pistachios, roasted unsalted peanuts, vacuum-packed cooked chestnuts, sesame seeds, raisins, dried sour cherries, prunes, dried cranberries

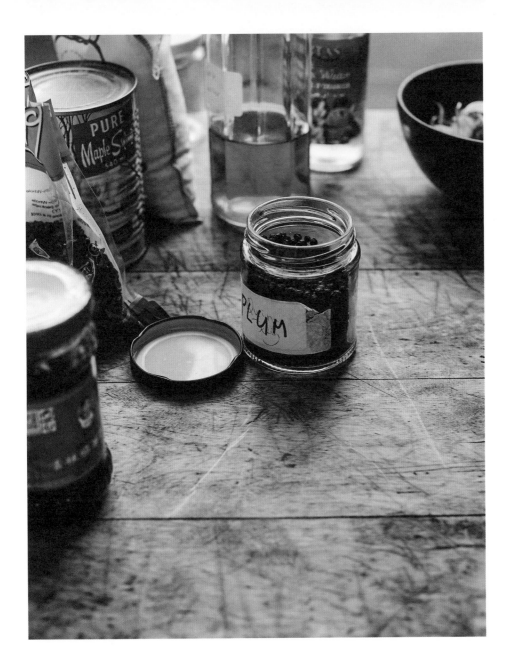

SWEET THINGS Honey, maple syrup, dark and light soft brown sugars, muscovado sugar, palm sugar, caster and granulated sugar

ALCOHOLS Amaretto, Marsala, amontillado sherry, dark rum, dry white vermouth, crème de cassis

BAKING Rose and orange flower waters, plain flour, self-raising flour, medium polenta, icing sugar, good-quality marzipan, dark chocolate (70% cocoa solids), cocoa powder, vanilla pods or vanilla extract, baking powder and bicarbonate of soda

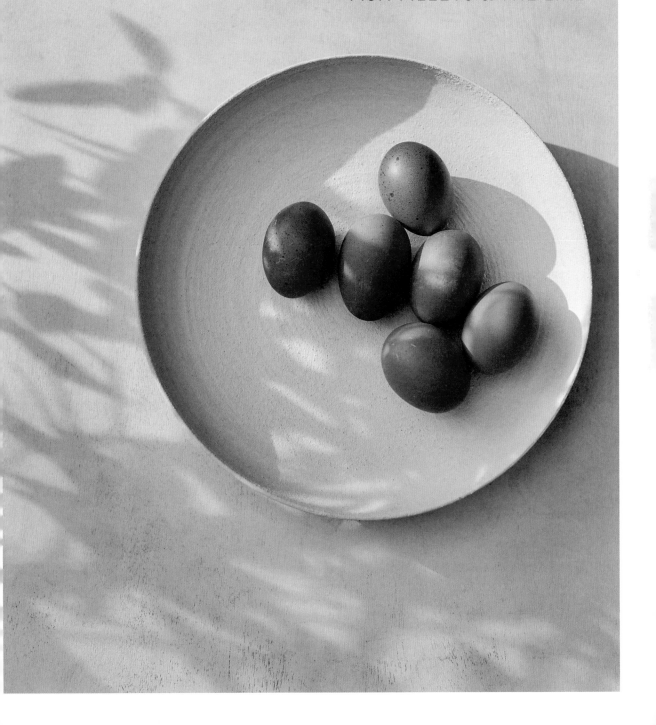

SIMPLE SUPPERS

SAUSAGES, CHOPS, FISH FILLETS & THE LIKE

BAKED SAUSAGES, APPLES & BLACKBERRIES WITH MUSTARD & MAPLE SYRUP

SERVES 4

8 good-quality chunky pork sausages

2 tart eating apples, halved (no need to peel or core)

2 medium onions, each cut into 6–8 wedges

2 rosemary sprigs

3½ tablespoons maple syrup

1½ tablespoons Dijon mustard

1 tablespoon extra virgin olive oil

2 garlic cloves, crushed

sea salt flakes and freshly ground black pepper

150ml (5fl oz) chicken stock

125g (4½oz) blackberries

mashed or baked potatoes, to serve

I know it's in the 'Simple Suppers' chapter, but this – glossy with blackberry juice and maple syrup – is special enough to give to friends at the weekend. I roast sausages all the time. Sometimes I brown them a little in a pan before transferring them to the oven; sometimes I just put them in the oven from raw, moistened with a little oil, and turn them halfway through cooking. Either way is infinitely less hassle than standing turning them over in a pan on the hob.

Preheat the oven to 190°C fan (400°F), Gas Mark 6.

Tumble the sausages, apples, onions and rosemary into a heavy flameproof roasting tin, shallow casserole or ovenproof frying pan about 30cm (12in) across, in which the ingredients can lie snugly in a single layer. There shouldn't be a lot of room around the ingredients or the juices will reduce and burn.

In a small bowl, stir together the maple syrup, mustard, olive oil and garlic, then pour this mixture into the pan. Season and turn the ingredients to coat them. Bake for 40–50 minutes, turning over the sausages once. They should be dark and glossy, with the apples completely soft.

Remove the tin, dish or pan from the oven and place over a medium-high heat, pouring in the stock. Bring almost to the boil, stirring to help the maple syrup and mustard mixture amalgamate with the stock. Add the blackberries to heat through (don't stir from now on, or they will break up) and serve with mashed or baked potatoes.

ROAST SALMON & GREEN BEANS WITH CORNICHONS & MUSTARD CRUMBS

They're not cheap, but salmon fillets do mean an easy supper, as they cook so quickly. Roast green beans were a revelation to me the first time I tried them (American chef and lover of vegetables, Joshua McFadden, got me into them). If you want to serve these beans as a side dish, roast them as directed here, scattering the flavoured crumbs over them at the end (and for more roast green beans, see pages 64 and 88).

Preheat the oven to 190°C fan (400°F), Gas Mark 6.

Put the green beans into a roasting tin or – even better – a shallow ovenproof dish that you would want to serve from, too. Toss them with a little of the oil and some seasoning.

Brush the salmon fillets with oil as well, season, then set them on top of the beans. Roast for 12 minutes.

Heat the remaining oil in a frying pan. When it's hot, add the breadcrumbs and fry briskly until golden, then add the garlic and cornichons and cook for another minute. Take the pan off the heat and stir in the mustard, parsley and lemon zest, mixing together well.

When 2 minutes of cooking time remain, spoon the breadcrumb mixture on top of the salmon and return it to the oven.

Squeeze the lemon juice over the top of the fish and serve.

SERVES 4

500g (1lb 2oz) green beans, topped but not tailed

4 tablespoons extra virgin olive oil

sea salt flakes and freshly ground black pepper

4 salmon fillets, 175–200g (6–7oz) each

50g (1¾oz) breadcrumbs from coarse white bread (such as ciabatta or sourdough)

1 garlic clove, finely grated

3 tablespoons drained and chopped cornichons

2 teaspoons Dijon mustard

2 tablespoons finely chopped flat leaf parsley leaves

finely grated zest and juice of ½ unwaxed lemon

TOAD IN THE HOLE WITH
LEEKS & CHEDDAR CHEESE

SERVES 4

3 large eggs

150g (5½oz) plain flour, sifted

125ml (4fl oz) whole milk

125ml (4fl oz) beer

1 tablespoon English mustard

sea salt flakes and freshly ground black pepper

45g (1½oz) beef dripping, or 2 tablespoons groundnut oil

8 good-quality pork sausages

18 baby leeks (not too fine), trimmed

55g (2oz) Cheddar cheese, coarsely grated

I wasn't brought up eating toad in the hole, so have no compunction about mucking around with it. Beer in the batter really helps it to rise, but the most important thing is to get the dripping or oil in your roasting tin as hot as possible, as that's what really helps it to puff up.

Beat the eggs with electric beaters until they're foamy and thick. Add the flour, then the milk and beer alternately, beating on a low speed, until everything is incorporated and the batter is smooth. Add the mustard and season well. Cover and leave to sit for 30 minutes.

Preheat the oven to 190°C fan (400°F), Gas Mark 6. Put half the dripping or oil in a heavy roasting tin (the one I use has a base measurement of 29 x 23cm / 11½ x 9in) and melt it over a medium heat. Add the sausages, turn them over in the fat, then roast for 10 minutes. Now add the leeks, turn both them and the sausages over in the fat and roast for another 10 minutes. Remove the leeks and sausages from the roasting tin.

Increase the oven temperature to 210°C fan (425°F), Gas Mark 7. Put the rest of the dripping or oil in the tin and, when the oven has reached the new hotter temperature, heat it until smoking.

Carefully remove the tin from the oven. Return the leeks to it, pour the batter on top, then return the sausages. Bake for another 20 minutes.

Take the roasting tin out, sprinkle on the cheese and return to the oven for a final 5 minutes. The batter should be puffed up and golden. Eat immediately.

SALSICCIA CON PATATE
E POMODORI AL FORNO

SERVES 4

8 chunky, spicy, good-quality Italian sausages

6 tablespoons extra virgin olive oil

¼ teaspoon chilli flakes (you may want more if your sausages aren't that spicy)

¼ teaspoon fennel seeds, bashed a bit in a mortar

2 onions, finely sliced

450g (1lb) potatoes, peeled and cut into slices about 3mm (⅛in) thick

3 garlic cloves, finely sliced

1 red and 1 yellow pepper, halved, deseeded and sliced

sea salt flakes and freshly ground black pepper

250g (9oz) tomatoes, sliced

30g (1oz) pecorino cheese, finely grated

2 tablespoons roughly chopped flat leaf parsley leaves, or the leaves from 4 oregano sprigs

This is great both for supper and as a weekend lunch. I don't know if it's particular to Sicily, though that's where I first ate it; it's such an obvious way to cook sausages and potatoes that I can't believe it's not done in other areas of Italy. You can use either waxy or floury potatoes; the floury variety will take a little less time to cook. (If you opt for small waxy potatoes, you don't need to peel them.) This calls for some peppery leaves on the side.

Preheat the oven to 190°C fan (400°F), Gas Mark 6.

Cut each sausage into 3 pieces. Heat 2 tablespoons of the olive oil in a wide, fairly shallow ovenproof pan, about 30cm (12in) in diameter. Quickly brown the sausages all over: you just want to get a bit of colour on the outside, not cook them through. Add the chilli and fennel and cook for another minute.

Toss in the onions, potatoes, garlic and peppers and season. Add another couple of tablespoons of olive oil, unless a lot of fat has come out of the sausages (some exude a lot, others don't). Finish with most of the sausage pieces on top.

Cook in the oven for 20 minutes. Take the dish out of the oven and stir everything round. Put the tomatoes on top, season, sprinkle on the cheese and drizzle on the remaining oil. Return to the oven and cook for a final 30–40 minutes, or until everything is golden and the potatoes are soft, gently stirring in whichever herb you want to use 10 minutes before the end of cooking time.

Serve in the dish in which it has been cooked.

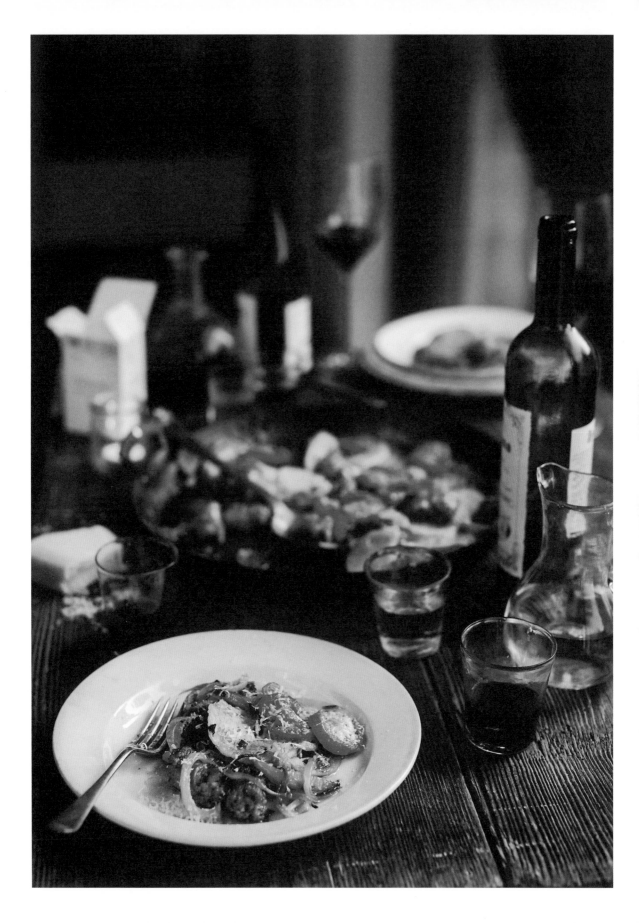

LAMB FILLET WITH HERB BUTTER, RADISHES & PEAS

SERVES 4

FOR THE HERB BUTTER

75g (2¾oz) unsalted butter, at room temperature

3 tablespoons chopped chervil or flat leaf parsley leaves mixed with chives

sea salt flakes and freshly ground black pepper

1 tablespoon dry white vermouth

FOR THE LAMB AND VEGETABLES

500g (1lb 2oz) frozen peas

25g (scant 1oz) unsalted butter

3 tablespoons extra virgin olive oil

150ml (5fl oz) dry white vermouth

150g (5½oz) spring onions, trimmed

300g (10½oz) radishes, halved lengthways

2 x 225g (8oz) lamb loin fillets, trimmed

squeeze of lemon juice

handful of mint leaves, torn

Sticking frozen peas in the oven? As Nigella Lawson has shown us (she has a genius recipe for baked chicken thighs with leeks and peas in her book, At My Table*), it works. The colour of the peas and the radishes together is beautiful. The butter is the gilding of the lily here, so just leave it out if you don't want to make it and, instead, throw herbs into the tin with the vegetables just before serving. Lamb fillet is expensive, so this isn't a Wednesday night dish, more a Friday treat.*

Preheat the oven to 190°C fan (400°F), Gas Mark 6.

To make the butter, just mash it with the herbs and seasoning, then slowly mash in the vermouth. You can put this in the fridge if you're making it in advance, otherwise it's fine to leave it at room temperature.

Put the peas into a 30cm (12in) shallow casserole or sauté pan with the regular butter (not the herb butter), 1 tablespoon of the olive oil, the vermouth and some seasoning. Cook in the oven for 25 minutes. After 10 minutes, toss the spring onions and radishes in another 1 tablespoon of the oil and season. Stir the peas, then throw the spring onions and radishes on top and return to the oven for their final 15 minutes.

Season the lamb with pepper and heat the last tablespoon of oil in an ovenproof frying pan over a very high heat. Brown the fillets all over, then transfer them – in the pan – to the oven for 10 minutes. Take them out, cover with foil and keep warm to let the meat rest for 10 minutes.

Squeeze some lemon juice into the peas and radishes and add the mint leaves. Slice the lamb and serve it – with a knob of herb butter melting over the top – with the peas and radishes.

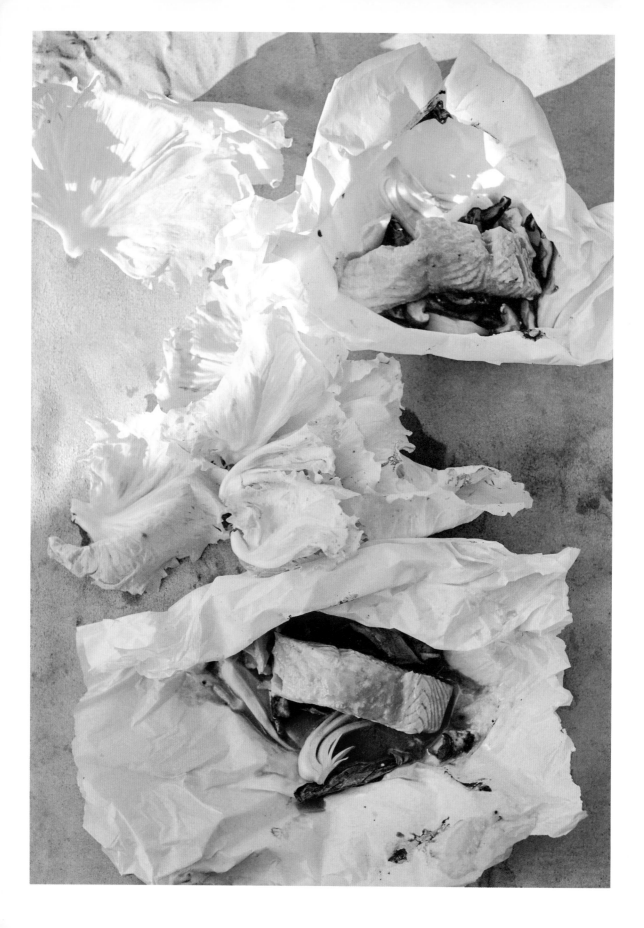

SALMON FILLETS WITH MISO, SHIITAKES & PAK CHOI

SERVES 4

2 tablespoons white miso paste

2 tablespoons runny honey

7 tablespoons Japanese rice wine (mirin), or dry vermouth or dry sherry

1 tablespoon light soy sauce

2 teaspoons peeled and finely grated fresh root ginger

2 teaspoons toasted sesame oil

a little groundnut oil

250g (9oz) shiitake mushrooms, trimmed and finely sliced

2 heads of pak choi, sliced lengthways

8 spring onions, trimmed and roughly chopped

4 thick salmon fillets (not skinny fillets from the tail)

a few sesame seeds (optional)

rice or noodles, to serve

Serving dishes en papillote – *in parcels* – *means that juices are created around whatever you're cooking. The paper parcels don't have to be neat – so don't labour over them – and use foil if you'd prefer (it's easier, but doesn't look as good). As this is quite a sweet dish, I like some bitter leaves – such as castelfranco, shown here, or endive – with it.*

Preheat the oven to 180°C fan (375°F), Gas Mark 5.

Mix together the miso, honey, 2 tablespoons of the rice wine, the soy sauce, ginger and sesame oil.

Put 4 rectangles of foil or baking parchment – each about 34 x 24cm (13½ x 9½in) and of double thickness – on to 1 or 2 baking sheets (depending on the size of the sheets). Brush the centre of each piece with groundnut oil.

Divide the mushrooms and pak choi between the pieces of foil, placing them in the centre (it will seem like a lot, but the vegetables really shrink as they cook). Sprinkle with the spring onions.

Drizzle about 1 tablespoon of the miso mixture over the top of each heap of vegetables, then set a salmon fillet on top. Spread the rest of the miso mixture on top of each piece of fish (use all of it).

Pull the foil or paper up around the salmon, enclosing the vegetables and nipping the ends of each parcel, but let the top of each fish fillet remain exposed. Spoon the remaining rice wine into each parcel, dividing it evenly.

Bake for 12 minutes. Sprinkle the salmon with sesame seeds, if you're using them, and serve the fish in the parcels, with rice or noodles on the side.

PORK CHOPS BAKED WITH BEETROOT, APPLES, CARAWAY & PAPRIKA

This is inspired by the flavours of Germany and Eastern Europe; it's a mixture of tastes and ingredients I love. Soured cream might seem a tad overindulgent (good chops have fat on them, so there's plenty of fat action going on), but even a small amount makes this dish sing, as it cuts the sweetness of the beetroot and apples.

Put the garlic into a mortar with the salt and caraway seeds and pound with the pestle. Add the olive oil, working it in until you have a rough paste. Put the pork chops in a bowl and add the mixture from the mortar, turning the chops over in it. Cover and marinate in the fridge for a while (at least 1 hour if possible, though longer is fine).

Preheat the oven to 180°C fan (375°F), Gas Mark 5.

Put everything for the vegetables into a gratin dish or a roasting tin in which the beetroot and apples can lie in a single layer. Toss around with your hands and bake in the oven for 10 minutes.

Heat a frying or griddle pan over a high heat until very hot. Add the chops and colour them on both sides, as well as on the fat (hold the chops on their sides, gripping them with tongs, so you can colour the fat). Season with pepper and a little more salt.

Put the chops on top of the vegetables and pour over the cooking juices from the frying pan. Bake for a final 20 minutes; the meat should be cooked through but still tender.

Transfer to a warmed serving dish, or serve in the dish in which it was cooked. Spoon some soured cream scattered with dill over the vegetables, or just serve it on the side.

SERVES 4

FOR THE PORK

4 garlic cloves, finely grated

sea salt flakes

4 teaspoons caraway seeds

2 tablespoons extra virgin olive oil

4 x 300g (10½oz) thick pork chops, on the bone

FOR THE VEGETABLES

500g (1lb 2oz) cooked beetroot, peeled and quartered

2 medium-sized tart eating apples, halved, cored and each cut into 12 wedges

2 onions, halved and sliced about 1cm (½in) thick

3 tablespoons extra virgin olive oil

4 tablespoons cider vinegar

1½ tablespoons soft light brown sugar

3 teaspoons paprika

¼ teaspoon chilli flakes

sea salt flakes and freshly ground black pepper

TO SERVE

soured cream

chopped dill (any coarse stalks discarded)

COD WITH CHORIZO, TOMATOES, OLIVES & SHERRY

SERVES 4

FOR THE COD AND CHORIZO

400g (14oz) baby potatoes, scrubbed and quartered

300g (10½oz) cherry tomatoes on the vine

115g (4oz) chorizo cooking sausages, sliced

leaves from 3 thyme sprigs, plus 3 whole thyme sprigs

sea salt flakes and freshly ground black pepper

3 tablespoons extra virgin olive oil

4 × 175g (6oz) thick cod fillets (not skinny fillets from the tail)

15g (½oz) good-quality green olives, unpitted

6 tablespoons amontillado sherry

lemon wedges, to serve

FOR THE CRUST

100g (3½oz) fresh white breadcrumbs

2 garlic cloves, crushed

finely grated zest of 1 small unwaxed lemon

1 tablespoon chopped flat leaf parsley leaves

leaves from 2 thyme sprigs

¼ teaspoon smoked paprika

60g (2¼oz) unsalted butter, melted

½ tablespoon amontillado sherry

It's funny to think that chorizo was once considered an exotic ingredient. We have taken the Spanish sausage so much to our hearts that it pops up everywhere (including where it has no business being). I love it, though, especially with fish and shellfish; its fatty smokiness is great with cod and mussels. This is a perfect all-in-one dish. Make sure to use the right kind of sherry (a too-sweet sherry will ruin this), though you could use fino instead of amontillado, if that's what you have.

Preheat the oven to 190°C fan (400°F), Gas Mark 6. Put all the vegetables, the chorizo and all the thyme into a roasting tin in which they can lie in a single layer. Season and add 2 tablespoons of the extra virgin olive oil (more oil will come out of the chorizo once it starts cooking). Toss everything around with your hands and roast in the oven for 30 minutes, turning the vegetables over a couple of times.

Now make the crust. Combine the breadcrumbs, garlic, lemon zest, herbs and smoked paprika and season well. Pour in the melted butter and sherry and mix with a large fork or your fingers until combined. Brush the cod fillets with the last tablespoon of oil, then cover them evenly with the crumbs, pressing down on them so they stick to the fish.

Mix the olives and sherry into the roasted vegetables and chorizo, then put the cod on top. Return to the oven and bake until the fish is cooked through: its flakes should be white, not glassy. This should take 15 minutes, but check for doneness and return the fish to the oven for no more than a couple of minutes if it needs a little longer. Serve with lemon wedges.

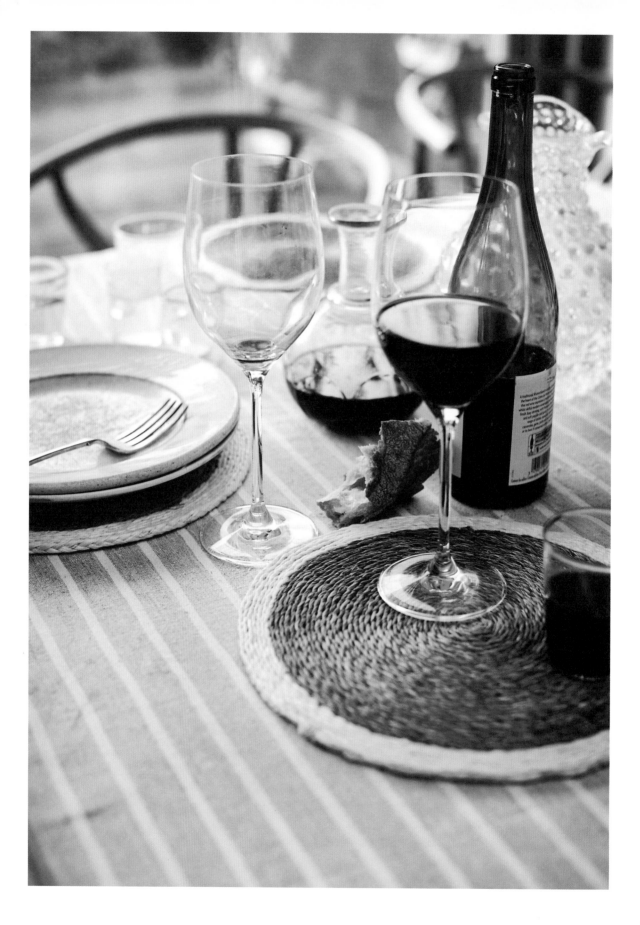

AT THE TABLE

I'm ticking off the items on my list scribbled, as usual, on the back of an envelope. The pears are lying in the pool of Marsala in which they've baked, and a glossy rubble of warm lentils with sausages on top has just come out of the oven. The table looks good. I've spent a lifetime collecting battered old cutlery and soft tablecloths and I love setting the table, even though I never do anything formal. There's just time to stick on a bit of lipstick – I rarely manage to change – before friends arrive. I feel a small thrill of excitement, but it's about the event rather than the food. Things happen at the table.

This is a book about getting dinner (or supper or whatever you call it) on the table every day, and about making food for friends. It's a cookbook. But a meal is always about more than the dishes served. Food isn't just physical sustenance, it's also about pleasure and about people. The 'table' in the title of this book is just as important as the 'oven'. I wanted to write the book so that home cooks – and people who aren't confident in the kitchen – could get good food on to that table with relative ease, so a good time could be had by everyone, including the cook.

Having friends over is a performance of sorts. Casualness is now *de rigueur*, but even casualness requires a bit of thought. Despite what I do for a living, I don't often have big crowds of people round to eat. I tend to cook for friends who are staying, or small groups. I do uphold the kitchen table's role in our lives on a daily basis, though, which is a challenge when your children are teenagers. I won't relinquish our meals together and I know that if I let them slide for a few days we are all less happy. Sitting at the table is where we look at each other. The table makes it impossible not to. Then we talk, and if the food is good we're happy. We also, it's true, argue. But we communicate and, in a time when everything can be texted or emailed or sent on WhatsApp, that's important. The table is under threat. We eat alone more, on the sofa, standing up in the kitchen, at our computers, on the go. We try to squash eating into busy lives.

Not all cultures sit round a table to eat (estimates suggest that about a quarter of the world's population eat around a mat) and we haven't always done it in the west either. I'm not going to pretend that meals taken at a table are always and everywhere happy. They've served as a very conservative force (think of that Norman Rockwell Thanksgiving painting where everyone is relentlessly smiling). The 1950s American educational film *A Date with Your Family* – you can watch it online – now looks shocking in its emphasis on the roles assigned for the evening meal. The mother and daughter change their clothes because, the narrator tells us, 'the women of this family seem to feel that they owe it to the men of the family to look relaxed, rested and attractive,' later adding, 'the table is no place for discontent'. It is, in fact, often a place of discontent. Many of the most memorable scenes in movies are about relationships collapsing at the table; in the Danish film, *Festen*, an entire extended family implodes, and in *American Beauty* the marriage between Lester and Carolyn Burnham bites the dust as the combatants fight across a table. A platter of asparagus ends up being thrown at the wall, the etiquette of the table literally smashed. If there are fault lines – in friendships, in marriages, in a family – the table is where they will be most evident.

But the table is, generally, a place where good things happen, or at least we hope they will. In 18th-century Dutch, a good friend is called a 'table friend'. When food is scarce – I'm particularly thinking of the meals that Russians put together when the country was part of the Soviet Union and it was hard to get hold of much – people try to create a feast that can be served at the table, even if it's just *salade Olivier* made with tinned vegetables and industrial mayonnaise, pickled cabbage, buckwheat and vodka.

In the last eighteen months – during the writing of this book – I've had more large groups of people over to eat than I've had in years, and have been strongly reminded of what magical things can happen over a table. The American writer Adam Gopnik has said, 'The test of a meal is the talk that it makes.' It's better if the food is good, of course – if you're bothering to have people over you want them to experience pleasure, that is your gift to them – but it can be good in an ordinary way. Things have changed. As a child in the 1970s, I used to pore over the cookery pages in my mum's magazines, mentally noting what I would eventually need to pull off a bit of entertaining when I grew up (basically a chignon and a hostess trolley). Then, in the 1980s – when I started cooking for friends in earnest – I served up ridiculously complicated *nouvelle cuisine* meals that took days to prepare. But once molecular gastronomy came along, we all stopped trying to be chefs in our homes (thank God), because none of us had the kit.

After a particular lovely lunch one Sunday (I served the chicken with orzo on page 175), my eldest child simply said: 'Let's do this more'. We'd invited old neighbours – a big sprawling garrulous family – and disparate friends who had just moved to London. People got to know each other simply by passing salt and bread, chairs were rearranged as small groups formed, noise levels were high, many jokes had been told, and I hadn't even bothered to serve the pudding 'nicely' (I brought the ice cream to go with the baked fruit to the table in its plastic tub). The food had been good, but not difficult or spectacular; everything had been transformed by the heat of the oven. As I looked at the mess when everyone had gone, words formed in my head, words that rang even truer than Gopnik's: 'Your reward for cooking is laughter,' I thought.

THYME-ROAST LAMB CHOPS WITH TOMATOES, BLACK OLIVES, POTATOES & GOAT'S CHEESE

Not an all-in-one dish, as you have to brown the chops and then put them on top of the vegetables, but even in the short period they're in the oven at the same time, the juices from the lamb flavour the potatoes, bringing both components together. The chops will take 10–12 minutes, depending on your oven. Keep an eye on them the first time you make this dish and then you'll know how long to cook them next time.

Put the chops in a dish with 2 tablespoons of the olive oil and half the thyme. Cover and leave to marinate for at least 1 hour, or in the fridge overnight.

When you're ready to cook, preheat the oven to 190°C fan (400°F), Gas Mark 6.

Put the potatoes, along with the tomatoes and onion, into a large gratin dish or a shallow casserole (about 30cm / 12in across is ideal) in which all the vegetables can lie in a single layer. Add the rest of the oil, some salt and pepper and the rest of the thyme. Separate the cloves of garlic and add those, too (you don't need to peel them). Toss everything together and roast in the oven for 25 minutes. Add the olives and scatter the goat's cheese over the top. Spoon on a little more oil. Return the dish to the oven for 10 minutes.

Heat a frying pan over a very high heat until really hot, season the chops and sear them until browned, about 1½ minutes on each side.

Put the chops on top of the vegetables and roast for a final 10 minutes, by which time they should be cooked through, but remain a little rare. The vegetables should be tender and the goat's cheese toasted on top.

SERVES 4

8 thick lamb loin chops

4 tablespoons extra virgin olive oil, plus a little more

leaves from 5 thyme sprigs, plus 3 whole thyme sprigs

450g (1lb) small waxy potatoes, scrubbed, halved or quartered, depending on size

330g (11½oz) cherry tomatoes

1 large red onion, cut into wedges

sea salt flakes and freshly ground black pepper

1 head of garlic

85g (3oz) good-quality black olives, pitted or not, as you prefer

150g (5½oz) goat's cheese, broken into rough chunks

CREAMY GRATIN OF SMOKED HADDOCK, TOMATOES & POTATOES

This recipe does take a bit of effort, because the potatoes have to be so finely sliced (a mandolin will save you a lot of time). You need a metal or cast-iron gratin dish, something that conducts heat well, otherwise it's difficult to cook the potatoes to tenderness in the time given.

Preheat the oven to 190°C fan (400°F), Gas Mark 6. Put a metal baking sheet in the oven to heat up.

Cut the fish into slices about 4cm (1½in) thick.

Slice the tomatoes finely. You don't need to save the juice, so leave whatever runs out on to the chopping board, as the slices shouldn't be too wet. Slice the potatoes finely too – you don't need to peel them, just scrub them well – using a mandolin if you have one. It's important that the slices are really wafer-thin or the potatoes won't cook through in the time given and you'll have to cook the gratin for longer, which means the fish will be overcooked.

Layer up half the potatoes and half the tomatoes in a metal gratin dish about 30cm (12in) in diameter, or an oval-shaped dish measuring 36 x 23cm (14½ x 9in), with a capacity of 2 litres (3½ pints), seasoning and sprinkling on the thyme as you do so.

Heat the cream and garlic to boiling, then strain it into a bowl and stir in the mustard, to taste. Pour half of the cream mixture over the vegetables.

Lay the fish on the cream-soaked vegetables, then add the rest of the vegetables and pour over the remaining hot cream. Sprinkle both cheeses on top.

Bake in the oven – sliding it on to the hot baking sheet – for 45–50 minutes, or until the potatoes are tender. Remove from the oven and leave to settle for 10 minutes, then serve.

SERVES 4–6

500g (1lb 2oz) smoked haddock fillets, skinned

400g (14oz) tomatoes

700g (1lb 9oz) waxy new potatoes, such as Charlotte

sea salt flakes and freshly ground black pepper

leaves from 6 thyme sprigs

500ml (18fl oz) double cream

1 garlic clove, sliced

1–2 teaspoons English mustard, to taste

40g (1½oz) extra-mature Cheddar cheese, grated

15g (½oz) Parmesan cheese, grated

SEARED & ROAST DUCK BREASTS WITH ASIAN-FLAVOURED PLUMS

SERVES 4

FOR THE PLUMS

550g (1lb 4oz) plums, halved and pitted

2 tablespoons runny honey

2½ tablespoons soft light brown sugar

1½ tablespoons soy sauce

2 broad strips of orange zest, plus juice of ½ orange

½ teaspoon ground ginger

½ teaspoon five spice

1½ teaspoons chilli flakes

2 garlic cloves, finely grated

sea salt flakes and freshly ground black pepper

FOR THE DUCK

4 duck breasts

The best way to cook duck breasts – and they make a handsome dinner (a bit of a treat) – is to 'sear-roast' them: the fat starts to melt in the pan on the hob, then the meat cooks in the oven. It produces much more consistent results than you get from cooking the duck solely on the hob. Perfect every time – these timings give you rare meat – and far less demanding than standing over a pan, continually turning the meat.

Preheat the oven to 180°C fan (375°F), Gas Mark 5.

Put everything for the plums into a roasting tin or ovenproof dish in which the plums can lie in a single layer, seasoning well with salt and pepper. Bake for 15 minutes, then turn the plums over and return to the oven to bake until they have completely collapsed (ripe plums may only need 20 minutes; really hard fruits could take as long as 35 minutes). Mash the cooked plums with a fork and taste for seasoning, then leave to cool.

Increase the oven temperature to 200°C fan (410°F), Gas Mark 6½.

Heat a large ovenproof frying pan and, when it's very hot, put the duck breasts in, skin side down. Cook until the fat starts to run out and the skin is seared and golden (3–4 minutes). Turn the breasts over and quickly cook them on the other side until coloured. Season all over. Put the pan into the oven and roast the duck for 7 minutes.

Cut into the underside of a duck breast to see how well it's done: you want them rare – but not raw – in the centre (if you don't like them very rare, cook for a little longer until they are the way you like them). Return them to the oven if they're not quite ready, though I wouldn't suggest you roast them for more than 10 minutes in total. When they're done, cover and set aside to rest for about 7 minutes so the juices can 'set'.

Carve the duck into slices and serve with the room-temperature plums.

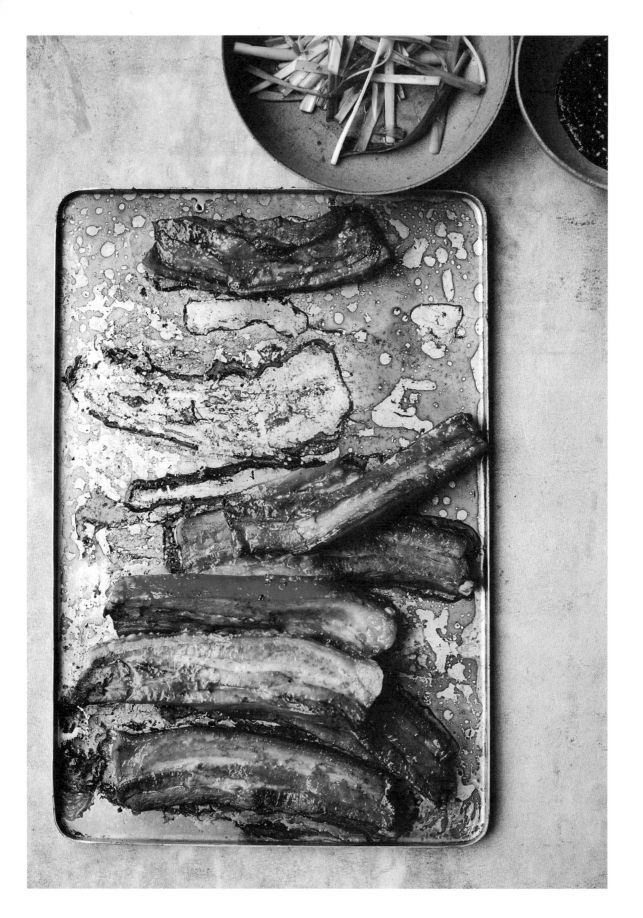

PORK BELLY STRIPS WITH SPRING ONION SALAD & KOREAN DIPPING SAUCE

This is based on a Korean dish called samgyeopsal-gui. *You can get both the Korean pastes online (larger supermarkets now stock them, too) and they have a good shelf life.*

Preheat the oven to 160°C fan (340°F), Gas Mark 3½.

Dry the pork belly slices with kitchen paper – if they're damp they won't brown – then put into a roasting tin large enough for them to lie in a single layer. Brush with oil, season and cook for about 90 minutes, turning the pork over twice during through the cooking time and pouring off the excess fat. When they're ready, they should be meltingly tender and golden brown, but sometimes, depending on your oven, they will need a quick blast at 210°C fan (425°F), Gas Mark 7, just until they become a good colour.

To make the dipping sauce, stir both the pastes together in a small bowl with the sesame oil, maple syrup or honey and garlic. Set aside.

For the salad, stir the soy sauce and sugar together in a small salad bowl until the sugar has dissolved, then mix in the sesame oil and chilli powder or chilli flakes to make a dressing.

Soak the spring onions in cold water for 5 minutes, then drain and dry. Halve them horizontally, then shred them lengthways, so that you end up with very fine slices. Toss the soy sauce dressing with the spring onions and sprinkle the sesame seeds on top.

Serve the meat with the dipping sauce, the spring onion salad and crispy vegetables: raw sticks of carrot and cucumber are good, as well as lettuce leaves (the crispness of Iceberg works well here).

SERVES 4

FOR THE PORK AND SAUCE

1.2kg (2lb 12oz) boneless pork belly slices, about 2cm (¾in) thick

a little groundnut oil

sea salt flakes and freshly ground black pepper

3 tablespoons *doenjang* soy bean paste

2 tablespoons *gochujang* chilli paste

2 tablespoons toasted sesame oil

2 tablespoons maple syrup or runny honey

2 garlic cloves, finely grated

carrot, cucumber and crisp lettuce, to serve

FOR THE SALAD

3 tablespoons soy sauce

2 teaspoons soft light brown sugar

2 tablespoons toasted sesame oil

½ teaspoon *gochugaru* (Korean sun-dried chilli powder), or ½ teaspoon regular chilli flakes

150g (5½oz) spring onions, trimmed

1 teaspoon sesame seeds

LAMB CHOPS WITH SWEET POTATOES, PEPPERS & MOJO VERDE

Mojo verde is Spanish for 'green sauce' and comes from the Canary Islands. There's also a red version and hundreds of variations on each (some more spicy than others, some more citrussy). I love the green sauce with sweet potatoes, pork, meaty fish and duck breast.

Put the lamb chops in a dish – or in a plastic food bag – with the cumin, some seasoning and half the olive oil. Cover (or seal) and put in the fridge while you get on with everything else.

Preheat the oven to 180°C fan (375°F), Gas Mark 5.

Put the sweet potatoes, onions and peppers into a roasting tin in which they can lie more or less in a single layer. Season and add the remaining oil. Toss the vegetables and roast for 30 minutes, turning them once during that time.

To make the *mojo verde*, put everything in a food processor and blitz. (You will have to push the ingredients down the sides of the bowl a couple of times.) Taste for seasoning.

Heat a frying pan over a high heat until really hot, then sear the chops over a very high heat until coloured, about 1½ minutes on each side.

Take the roasting tin out of the oven and put the chops on top of the vegetables. Return to the oven and cook for a final 10 minutes, by which time the chops should be cooked through, but remain a little rare.

Serve the lamb chops and vegetables with the *mojo verde*.

SERVES 4

FOR THE LAMB AND VEGETABLES

8 thick lamb loin or chump chops

1 teaspoon ground cumin

sea salt flakes and freshly ground black pepper

5 tablespoons extra virgin olive oil

650g (1lb 7oz) sweet potatoes, peeled, or scrubbed and unpeeled, as you prefer, cut into chunks

2 medium onions, cut into slim wedges

2 red peppers, halved, deseeded and cut into broad strips

FOR THE MOJO VERDE

3 garlic cloves, chopped

1 green pepper, halved, deseeded and chopped

5 tablespoons extra virgin olive oil

2 tablespoons white wine vinegar

1 teaspoon ground cumin

100g (3½oz) coriander leaves

STEAK WITH SOY-GINGER BUTTER

SERVES 4

FOR THE BUTTER

100g (3½oz) unsalted
butter, at room temperature

4 spring onions, trimmed and
finely chopped

1.5cm (⅝in) fresh root
ginger, peeled and
finely grated

2 tablespoons soy sauce

FOR THE STEAK

groundnut oil, or beef
dripping, if you have it

4 x 250g (9oz) sirloin steaks,
each about 3cm (1¼in) thick

sea salt flakes and freshly
ground black pepper

*This method for cooking steak – searing over a very high heat, then
transferring to the oven – might seem unorthodox, but I learned
it from chef Neil Rankin, who knows a thing or two about meat
cookery. It works every time. He doesn't even rest the steaks after
cooking them like this (the juices don't run out when you cut into
the meat). If you have cast-iron frying pans that can go in the oven,
use those, so you won't have to transfer the steaks to a roasting tin or
baking sheet. This makes more butter than you need, but it's hard to
work with smaller quantities: try it on fish or corn cobs. I even like
it on toast (deliciously umami).*

Mash the butter with the spring onions, ginger and soy sauce, gradually working
in the soy sauce until amalgamated. You can leave this at room temperature or
put it in the fridge. Some people like to chill the butter a little, then shape it into
a log and wrap it in greaseproof paper, so you can cut it into rounds. (I hate how
long it takes the cold butter to melt, so I prefer it at room temperature.)

Preheat the oven to 140°C fan (300°F), Gas Mark 2. Put in an empty roasting tin
or metal baking sheet to heat up, large enough to hold all the steaks.

Heat 1 large frying pan (or 2 smaller ones) – cast iron, if possible – for
7–10 minutes. Add a tiny bit of oil or dripping. Once it smokes, it is ready.

Put the steaks into the pan. First hold the fat of each of them against the base of the
pan to render it a little and add colour – you need to grip each steak with tongs as
you do this – then lay the steaks flat and press down with your tongs. Season and
flip the steaks over frequently, moving them round the pan and making sure you
can hear them sizzle. If the pan gets too hot – and the steak is becoming too dark –
reduce the heat (you want a good colour, but not burned meat).

Once the surfaces are well coloured – this should take about 4 minutes – transfer
the steaks to the hot roasting tin or baking sheet in the oven. Finish cooking the
steaks in the oven: 2 minutes for rare, 5 minutes for medium-rare.

Serve the steaks with a knob of the soy-ginger butter melting over the top.

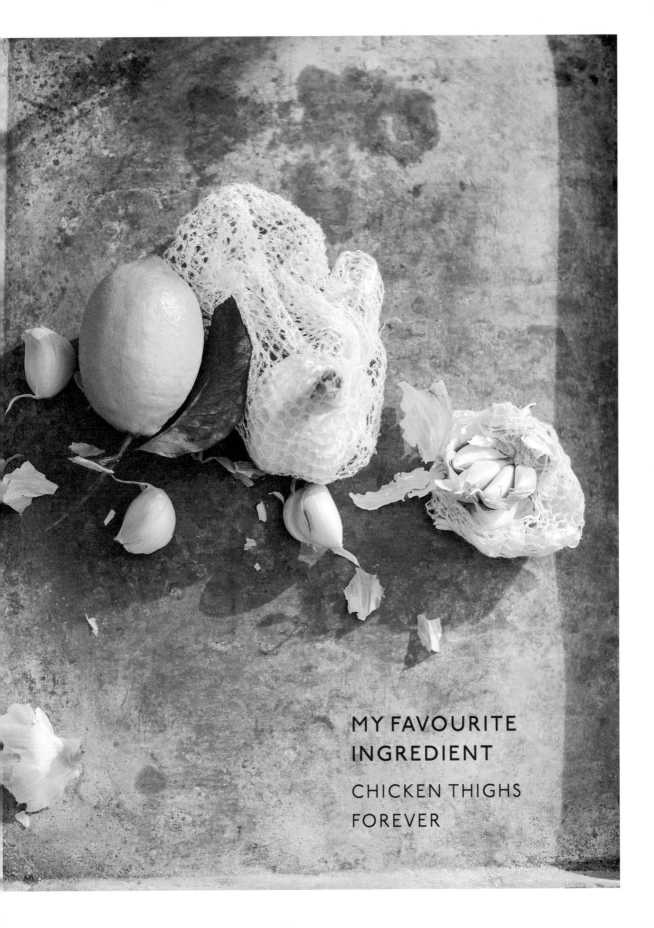

MY FAVOURITE
INGREDIENT

CHICKEN THIGHS
FOREVER

CHICKEN WITH FETA CHEESE, DILL, LEMON & HARISSA YOGURT

SERVES 4

450g (1lb) small waxy potatoes, scrubbed and quartered

2 red onions, halved and cut into wedges

1 head of garlic, cloves separated but not peeled

3 tablespoons extra virgin olive oil

sea salt flakes and freshly ground black pepper

8 good-sized skin-on bone-in chicken thighs, excess skin neatly trimmed

finely grated zest of 1 unwaxed lemon, plus juice of ½ lemon

75–100g (2¾–3½oz) feta cheese, crumbled

10g (¼oz) dill leaves, torn

250g (9oz) Greek yogurt

1 tablespoon harissa

All the dishes in this chapter are made with chicken thighs, because I unashamedly love them. They're succulent – so much better than breasts, which can dry out, in fact it's hard to overcook chicken thighs – they all cook at the same time (and quickly) and there's no carving. If you like a mixture of thighs and drumsticks, all the recipes on the pages that follow will work with those, too, just replace half the thighs in any dish with drumsticks. Lots of the relishes on pages 206–207 would work with roast chicken thighs, just cook the meat as below, leaving out the feta cheese, dill and lemon, and serve it with a relish instead.

Preheat the oven to 190°C fan (400°F), Gas Mark 6.

Put the potatoes, onions, garlic cloves, 2 tablespoons of the oil, salt and pepper into a 30cm (12in) wide shallow casserole or ovenproof sauté pan. Toss everything around with your hands. Put the chicken thighs on top, skin side up. Brush the remaining oil on the chicken and season it.

Roast for 40–45 minutes, or until the chicken is golden and the potatoes tender when pierced with a sharp knife.

Squeeze the lemon juice over, then scatter on the zest, feta and dill.

Put the yogurt into a bowl and spoon the harissa on top. Serve the chicken with the harissa yogurt on the side.

CHICKEN WITH MISO, SWEET POTATOES & SPRING ONIONS

This is my 'Lost in Translation' dish. I don't know that much about Japanese food, but you start with any cuisine by feeling your way, then gradually you fall for its flavours. I have come to love miso and the big umami punch it delivers, especially when used with sweet ingredients.

Preheat the oven to 190°C fan (400°F), Gas Mark 6.

Put the chicken thighs or joints into a big roasting tin with the sweet potato wedges (they should be able to lie – more or less – in a single layer).

In a small bowl, mix everything else together, except the spring onions and sesame seeds. Pour this over the chicken and sweet potatoes, turning everything over so the ingredients get well coated. Finish with the chicken skin side up.

Roast for 45 minutes, basting every so often and turning the sweet potato wedges over.

Stir the ingredients for the final basting together in another small bowl.

About 15 minutes before the end of cooking time, take the tin out of the oven, add the spring onions and pour the final basting mixture over everything. Return to the oven. The spring onions should become soft and slightly charred.

Transfer the chicken and vegetables to a warmed platter and sprinkle with the sesame seeds. Serve immediately, with stir-fried green vegetables.

SERVES 4–6

FOR THE CHICKEN

8 good-sized skin-on bone-in chicken thighs, excess skin neatly trimmed

700g (1lb 9oz) sweet potatoes, scrubbed and cut into wedges

2½ tablespoons white miso paste

1½ tablespoons runny honey

2 tablespoons sake, or dry sherry

1 tablespoon dark soy sauce

2.5cm (1in) fresh root ginger, peeled and finely grated

3 garlic cloves, finely grated

1 red chilli, halved and finely chopped (use the seeds)

12–18 spring onions, trimmed

3 teaspoons black or toasted white sesame seeds (or a mixture of both)

stir-fried green vegetables, to serve

FOR THE FINAL BASTING

1 tablespoon white miso paste

1 tablespoon runny honey

½ tablespoon dark soy sauce

½ tablespoon sake, or dry sherry

CHICKEN WITH PLUMS, HONEY & POMEGRANATES

Try to find crimson-fleshed plums, as they look stunning, and use walnuts instead of pistachios in the relish for a change (walnuts lend a slightly sweet-bitter, woody flavour). Couscous or bulgur wheat and a bowl of Greek yogurt are good on the side. This is cooked at a slightly lower temperature than the other chicken thigh recipes, because honey can burn if the heat is too high. If the skin is getting very dark, cover the roasting tin with foil.

Preheat the oven to 180°C fan (375°F), Gas Mark 5.

Put the chicken thighs into a 30cm (12in) ovenproof dish or shallow casserole in which they can all lie in a single layer. Add the sumac, ground coriander, half the garlic and all the olive oil and season. Turn everything over with your hands to make sure it's coated, then cover and marinate in the fridge for 1 hour, if you have the time. Mix the onions with the chicken and the marinade, then arrange the thighs so they are skin side up. Dot half the plums among the chicken.

In a small bowl, stir the honey and pomegranate molasses together with the cayenne pepper, cumin, orange zest and the remaining garlic. Spoon half of this over the chicken and plums. Sprinkle half the sugar on the plums and season them, then pour the orange juice around.

Roast for 25 minutes, then spoon the rest of the honey and pomegranate molasses over the chicken skin. Add the remaining plums and sprinkle them with the remaining sugar. Return to the oven to cook for a final 20 minutes.

For the relish, bash the nuts in a mortar with the garlic and some salt. Add the coriander and bash a bit more to break it all down a bit, not grind it to a paste, then stir in the olive oil and lemon juice. Season to taste, then spoon it over the chicken and scatter with pomegranate seeds.

SERVES 4

FOR THE CHICKEN

8 good-sized skin-on bone-in chicken thighs, excess skin neatly trimmed

2 teaspoons sumac

1 teaspoon ground coriander

4 garlic cloves, finely grated

3 tablespoons extra virgin olive oil

sea salt flakes and freshly ground black pepper

2 red onions, cut into fine crescent moon-shaped slices

8 plums (preferably crimson-fleshed and firm), halved and pitted

4 tablespoons runny honey

3 tablespoons pomegranate molasses

½ teaspoon cayenne pepper

1½ teaspoons ground cumin

finely grated zest of ½ orange

4 teaspoons soft light brown sugar

50ml (2fl oz) orange juice

3 tablespoons pomegranate seeds

FOR THE PISTACHIO RELISH

25g (scant 1oz) shelled unsalted pistachio nuts, chopped

1 garlic clove, finely chopped

3 tablespoons chopped coriander leaves

1 tablespoon extra virgin olive oil

lemon juice, to taste

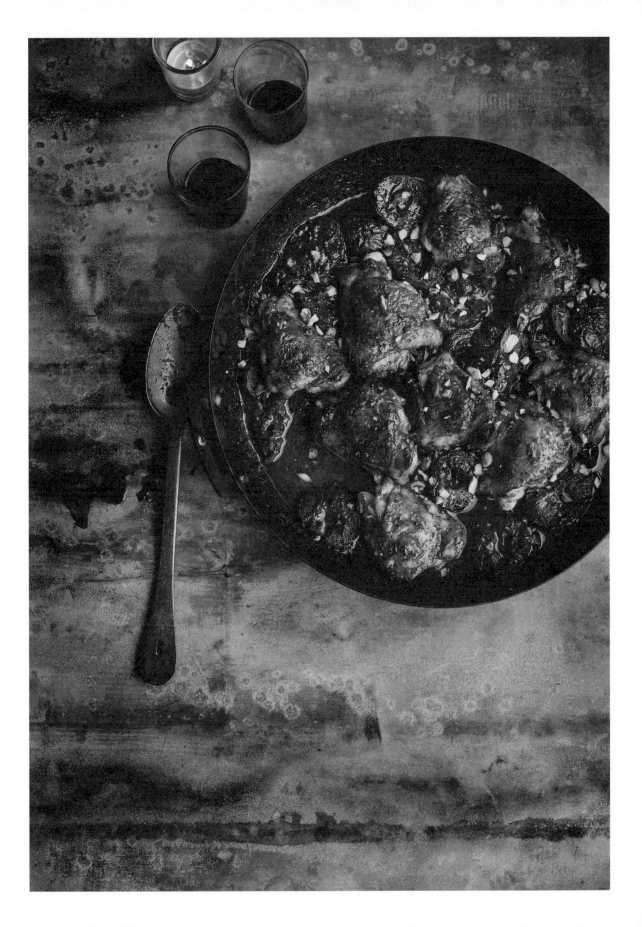

CHICKEN WITH LEMON, CAPERS & THYME

SERVES 4

550g (1lb 4oz) small waxy potatoes, scrubbed and halved or quartered, depending on size

2 onions, cut into crescent moon-shaped wedges

1 head of garlic, cloves separated but not peeled

10 thyme sprigs

2 unwaxed lemons

3 tablespoons extra virgin olive oil

sea salt flakes and freshly ground black pepper

8 good-sized skin-on bone-in chicken thighs, excess skin neatly trimmed

3 tablespoons capers, drained, rinsed and patted dry

This is simplicity itself, but you still have to take care: if you put the lemon slices on top from the start they'll burn, so keep them tucked away under the chicken and vegetables until you get near the end of cooking time. Green or black olives could also be added about five minutes before the end. This dish would be lovely with Baked peppers stuffed with goat's cheese, ricotta & basil (see page 77); you can cook them in the oven at the same time.

Preheat the oven to 190°C fan (400°F), Gas Mark 6.

Put the potatoes into a shallow casserole 30cm (12in) across, or into a roasting tin in which all the vegetables can lie in a single layer. Add the onions, garlic cloves and thyme. Finely grate the zest of 1 lemon over this and squeeze on the juice of half of it. Cut the other lemon into fine slices (flick out any seeds you see).

Add 2 tablespoons of the extra virgin olive oil to the vegetables and season them. Toss the lemon slices in and turn everything over with your hands.

Put the chicken thighs on top, skin side up, and brush them with the remaining olive oil. Season them, too. Make sure no lemon slices are sticking out, as they will burn quickly; they should be tucked under the chicken.

Roast in the oven for 30 minutes. Retrieve some of the lemon slices and put them on top of the chicken, so they can turn golden in the last bit of cooking time. Scatter the capers over and return to the oven for a final 10 minutes. Serve straight away.

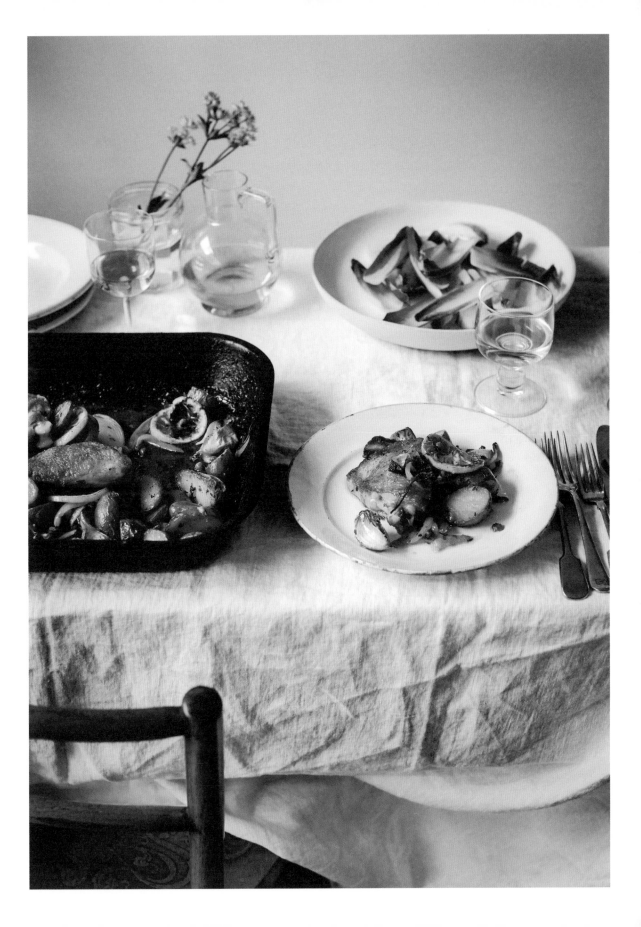

CHICKEN WITH HOT SAUSAGES & RED PEPPERS

SERVES 6–8

3 tablespoons extra virgin olive oil

8 good-sized skin-on bone-in chicken thighs, excess skin neatly trimmed

400g (14oz) good-quality spicy Italian sausages

3 red peppers

2 red onions, halved and cut into crescent moon-shaped slices

1 teaspoon chilli flakes

8 garlic cloves, finely grated

sea salt flakes and freshly ground black pepper

2 tablespoons sherry vinegar

leaves from 1 rosemary sprig, plus 3 whole rosemary sprigs

olive oil-roasted potatoes, mashed potatoes, or rice pilaf, to serve

Chicken thighs can vary a lot in size. For this to feed eight, you need big pieces; it will feed fewer if the thighs are on the small side. Try to find good-quality Italian sausages, the type that are flavoured with chilli or fennel are good for this.

Preheat the oven to 180°C fan (375°F), Gas Mark 5.

Heat half the olive oil in a big shallow casserole in which the thighs can lie in a single layer, or use a heavy roasting tin that can go on the hob and in the oven. Quickly brown the chicken on both sides – you don't want to cook it through, just get some colour on it – then remove from the pan. Do the same with the sausages, colouring them all over.

Cut the sausages on the diagonal into pieces. Halve and deseed the peppers and cut each half into 4 pieces lengthways.

Toss the peppers and onions into the casserole or roasting tin with the chilli flakes, garlic, seasoning, the rest of the oil, the sherry vinegar, rosemary and sausages. Turn everything over with your hands. Put the chicken, skin side up, on top of this.

Bake in the oven for 40–45 minutes, turning the vegetables over a couple of times. The chicken should be cooked through. Serve either with little potatoes that you've roasted in olive oil (*see* pages 107–109), or with mashed potatoes, or rice pilaf (mash or pilaf scented and coloured with a little saffron would be lovely with this).

CHICKEN WITH DIJON MUSTARD, CRÈME FRAÎCHE & VERMOUTH

SERVES 4

8 good-sized skin-on bone-in chicken thighs, excess skin neatly trimmed

4 tablespoons Dijon mustard

1 tablespoon extra virgin olive oil

freshly ground black pepper

½ garlic clove, finely grated

6 tablespoons crème fraîche

150ml (5fl oz) dry white vermouth

2 tablespoons very finely chopped flat leaf parsley leaves

squeeze of lemon juice

10g (¼oz) chilled unsalted butter, chopped

This recipe shows precisely how roasting – with a little liquid underneath the chicken – can produce a better dish than sautéing. Here, a lovely sauce is created below the chicken as it cooks, while its skin ends up with a lovely golden 'crust' on top. I've adapted the dish from one in Molly Stevens's All About Roasting. *If you're into roasting, it's a must-have book (though it's American, so you have to convert the quantities).*

Preheat the oven to 190°C fan (400°F), Gas Mark 6.

Put the chicken thighs into a heavy roasting tin in which they can lie in a single layer, sitting snugly together with not much room around them, or into a 30cm (12in) shallow casserole.

In a small bowl, mix the mustard with the olive oil and spread this all over the skin of the chicken. Season with pepper (there's a lot of salt in the Dijon mustard). Mix the garlic with the crème fraîche and dollop it on top of the chicken (it doesn't have to be neat, as it will melt and run off the chicken once it goes into the oven). Pour in about 100ml (3½fl oz) of the vermouth, at the sides, so it runs underneath the chicken.

Cook for 40 minutes, adding the rest of the vermouth halfway through.

Put the chicken on to a warmed plate and cover it with foil and a couple of tea towels to keep it warm.

Quickly bring the juices in the tin or casserole to the boil and reduce them a little so that they thicken. Add the parsley and lemon juice and whisk in the butter, bit by bit. Return the chicken to the sauce, then serve.

CHICKEN WITH TORN SOURDOUGH, SHERRY, RAISINS & BITTER LEAVES

There's a lot going on here, though it's a very simple dish. The sourdough pieces end up crunchy with a moist, slightly boozy, garlic-infused underside, there is sweetness from the sherry and raisins, bitterness from the leaves and saltiness from the bacon. It's all about contrast. Use watercress – just arrange small fistfuls among the cooked chicken – if you aren't keen on bitter leaves, and up the chilli if you want more heat.

Preheat the oven to 190°C fan (400°F), Gas Mark 6.

Put the bread, potatoes, onion, thyme, chilli and garlic cloves into a large roasting tin. Cut the pancetta or bacon into meaty chunks and add them to the tin with the chicken. Pour on the sherry vinegar, 70ml (2½fl oz) of the sherry and 4 tablespoons olive oil. Season and toss everything round with your hands, finishing with the chicken skin side up. Make sure the bread isn't too exposed, or lying at the edges, or it will become too dark.

Roast for 25 minutes – tossing the ingredients round once, but making sure the chicken is still skin side up – then add another 50ml (2fl oz) sherry.

Mix the spring onions in a bowl with the remaining olive oil and add them to the tin, too, laying them on top of the vegetables. Return to the oven and roast for a final 15 minutes.

Pour the remaining sherry into a small saucepan with the raisins and bring to just under the boil. Leave these to sit, then add them to the roasting tin 5 minutes before the end of the cooking time.

Transfer everything to a large warmed platter or broad shallow serving dish (unless you're happy to take the roasting tin to the table) and mix in whichever of the leaves you want to use (or just serve them on the side). Throw on the pine nuts and serve.

SERVES 4

175g (6oz) sourdough bread, torn into pieces roughly 5cm (2in) square

450g (1lb) small waxy potatoes, scrubbed and cut into chunks

1 large onion, cut into wedges

6 thyme sprigs

2 teaspoons chilli flakes

1 head of garlic, cloves separated but not peeled

150g (5½oz) pancetta or bacon, in 1 piece

8 good-sized skin-on bone-in chicken thighs, excess skin neatly trimmed

2 tablespoons sherry vinegar

220ml (8fl oz) amontillado sherry

5 tablespoons extra virgin olive oil

sea salt flakes and freshly ground black pepper

150g (5½oz) spring onions, trimmed

50g (1¾oz) raisins

100g (3½oz) bitter salad leaves (such as radicchio, chicory, curly endive, dandelion or treviso)

25g (scant 1oz) toasted pine nuts

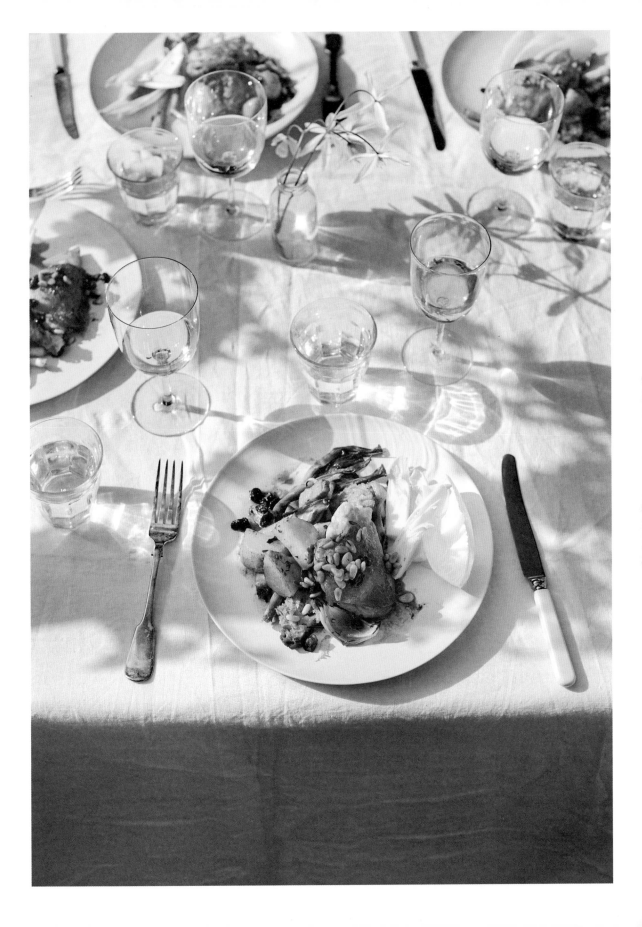

CHICKEN & CAULIFLOWER
WITH 'NDUJA

The work here is done in about eight minutes flat and the end result is totally moreish. I cook this a lot. You need to toss the elements around a few times during the cooking – to make sure the cauliflower colours all over – but that's it. Add red onion wedges, too, if you want. 'Nduja is a spicy, spreadable Calabrian salami; get it online or from good Italian delis.

Preheat the oven to 190°C fan (400°F), Gas Mark 6.

Put all the ingredients in a roasting tin or a broad, shallow casserole about 30cm (12in) across, season and toss around with your hands. The chicken should finish skin side up. Make sure the nuggets of 'nduja aren't lying on top, or they'll burn.

Roast for 40–45 minutes, turning everything over about 3 times during the cooking. The 'nduja partly melts and you need to ensure it gets well mixed in.

Towards the end of the cooking time, it's good to spoon the bits of 'nduja over the chicken, as it gives it a lovely colour. The potatoes should be tender when pierced with a sharp knife and the chicken cooked through. Serve with a green salad or bitter leaves.

SERVES 4

8 good-sized skin-on bone-in chicken thighs, excess skin neatly trimmed

1 medium cauliflower, broken into florets

450g (1lb) baby waxy potatoes, scrubbed, then halved or quartered, depending on size

75g (2¾oz) 'nduja, broken into nuggets

6 thyme sprigs

3 tablespoons olive oil

sea salt flakes and freshly ground black pepper

green salad, or bitter leaves, to serve

CHICKEN WITH PRUNES, POTATOES, CAULIFLOWER & HARISSA

The flavours of a tajine without the fuss. This is quite sweet, because of the prunes, so it does need the preserved lemon to cut through that. If you don't like prunes (I know they divide people), use dried apricots or pitted dates instead.

Preheat the oven to 190°C fan (400°F), Gas Mark 6.

In a bowl, mix together the harissa, spices, garlic, sugar, salt and pepper and olive oil.

Cut the potatoes – there's no need to peel them – into 2mm (¹⁄₁₆in) slices and put them into a shallow 30cm (12in) casserole with the onions. Add the cauliflower and prunes. Take one-third of the harissa mixture and toss it with this. Add the chicken stock and place over a medium heat until the mixture is simmering.

Remove the flesh from the preserved lemons – keep the rind for scattering on top – chop it, then add it to the rest of the harissa mixture, along with the brine from the jar. Mix the chicken thighs with this mixture, rubbing it all over. Set the chicken on top of the simmering vegetables, skin side up. Season the chicken skin and put the dish into the oven.

Cook for 45 minutes, taking the dish out and scooping the cooking juices up over the chicken a couple of times. You should end up with dark golden chicken and tender vegetables.

Cut the preserved lemon rind into shreds and throw it over the dish along with the coriander. This is good with a nut relish (*see* page 50), made with pistachios or walnuts. If you want to serve a grain on the side, *see* pages 150–151 for some ideas. A bowl of Greek yogurt – you can grate some garlic into it or leave it as it is – is excellent, though.

SERVES 4

2½ tablespoons harissa

1 teaspoon ground turmeric

1 teaspoon ground ginger

½ teaspoon ground cinnamon

1 teaspoon ground cumin

4 garlic cloves, finely grated

1 tablespoon soft light brown sugar

sea salt flakes and freshly ground black pepper

2 tablespoons extra virgin olive oil

400g (14oz) small waxy potatoes, scrubbed

2 onions, sliced

375g (13oz) cauliflower florets (about ½ large head)

about 12 moist prunes (more is fine)

300ml (½ pint) chicken stock

2 preserved lemons, plus 1½ tablespoons brine from the jar

8 good-sized skin-on bone-in chicken thighs, excess skin neatly trimmed

3 tablespoons roughly chopped coriander leaves

Pistachio relish, to serve (optional, see page 48)

Greek yogurt, to serve

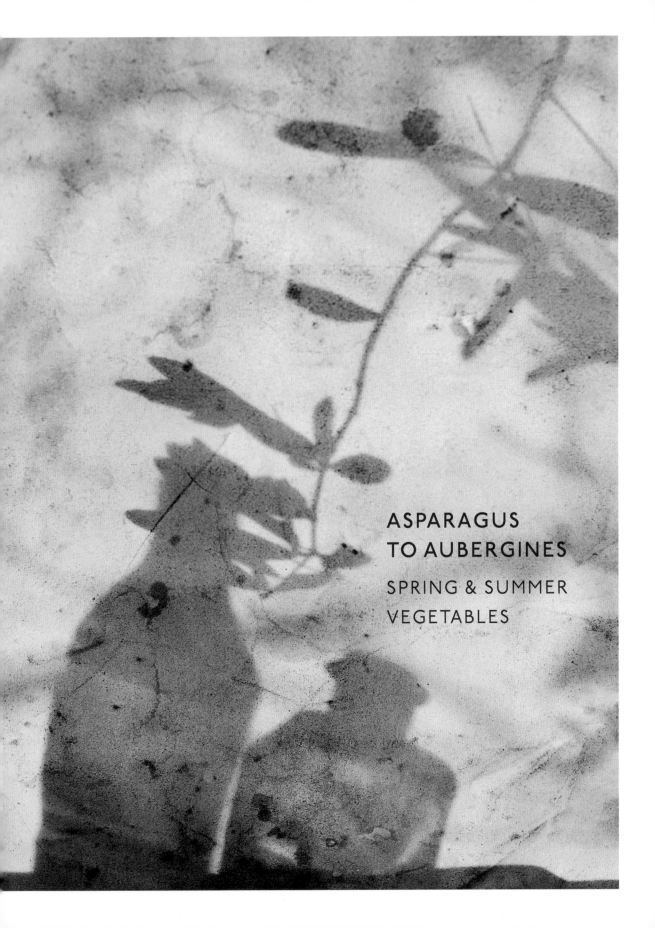

ASPARAGUS
TO AUBERGINES

SPRING & SUMMER
VEGETABLES

CUMIN-ROAST GREEN BEANS & TOMATOES WITH TAHINI & CORIANDER

If you've never roasted green beans, you've been missing out. They stay a little crisp, wrinkle ever so slightly and have a more intense flavour than beans cooked in (or over) water. You need to pay attention to timings, though. The beans can turn from perfect to overdone quite suddenly.

Preheat the oven to 190°C fan (400°F), Gas Mark 6.

Put the tomatoes into a roasting tin or on a baking sheet that has a lip all the way around. There needs to be room to add the beans later. Toss the tomatoes with 1 tablespoon of the oil and season them well. Roast in the oven for 10 minutes.

Toss the green beans in a bowl with the remaining 1 tablespoon of oil and the cumin seeds. Scatter the beans on top and around the tomatoes. Return to the oven for a final 10 minutes. At the end of the roasting time, the tomatoes should be completely soft and the beans slightly scorched.

To make the dressing, mix all the ingredients together in a bowl and season well. The tahini will 'seize' and thicken when you add the lemon juice, but don't worry, it will break down again when you add the water and beat hard with a wooden spoon. Tahini varies in thickness, so you might need more water than I've suggested here to achieve a dressing as thick as single cream.

Spoon the dressing on a plate, place the vegetables on top and scatter with the sesame seeds and coriander. You can serve this at room temperature, though I prefer it slightly warm.

FOR THE VEGETABLES

500g (1lb 2oz) cherry tomatoes on the vine, mixed colours if possible

2 tablespoons extra virgin olive oil

sea salt flakes and freshly ground black pepper

500g (1lb 2oz) green beans, topped but not tailed

1½ teaspoons cumin seeds

2 teaspoons sesame seeds

2 tablespoons roughly chopped coriander leaves

FOR THE TAHINI DRESSING

75g (2¾oz) tahini

juice of ½ lemon

5 tablespoons water, plus more if needed

2 garlic cloves, finely grated

4 tablespoons extra virgin olive oil

1½ teaspoons runny honey

FOR THE AUBERGINES
6 medium-large aubergines

a little extra virgin olive oil

black sesame seeds, to serve

natural yogurt, to serve

FOR THE BUTTER
good pinch of saffron
threads

6 black cardamom pods

60g (2¼oz) unsalted butter,
at room temperature

4 Medjool dates, pitted
and chopped

2 garlic cloves, crushed

¼ teaspoon cayenne pepper,
or to taste

generous pinch of ground
ginger, or to taste

sea salt flakes, to taste

WHOLE AUBERGINES WITH SAFFRON, BLACK CARDAMOM & DATE BUTTER

It seems odd to pair aubergines with butter – we more often think of them being cooked with oil – but ghee is used with them in Indian cookery, so why not? Butter can really melt into cooked aubergine; in fact, I think the flesh soaks it up better than oil. I use black cardamom – which has a smoky, slightly meaty flavour – in the butter here, but you can use green cardamom, though the results are quite different. With soft bread – naan is best – and yogurt flavoured with coriander and garlic, this makes a meal.

Preheat the oven to 190°C fan (400°F), Gas Mark 6.

For the butter, put the saffron into a small bowl or cup and add ½ tablespoon boiling water. Stir, then leave to cool. Break the cardamom pods open and remove the seeds. Grind them as well as you can with a mortar and pestle.

Put the butter into a bowl, add the saffron and cardamom and stir and mash to combine well. Add the dates, garlic, cayenne and ginger and season well with salt. Stir and mash to combine again, then taste: you may want more cayenne or ginger, but these spices shouldn't overwhelm the cardamom. Shape the butter into a log and wrap it in greaseproof paper, or just transfer it to a bowl and cover it. Either way, it needs to go into the fridge (because of the dates, this is better a little chilled).

Put the aubergines in a roasting tin and brush lightly with some of the oil. Pierce each one a few times with the tines of a fork. Roast for 40–45 minutes, or until the aubergines are completely soft and look a bit deflated.

Slit the aubergines down the middle. Add knobs of the spiced date butter and allow it to melt. Sprinkle on sesame seeds and serve with a bowl of yogurt.

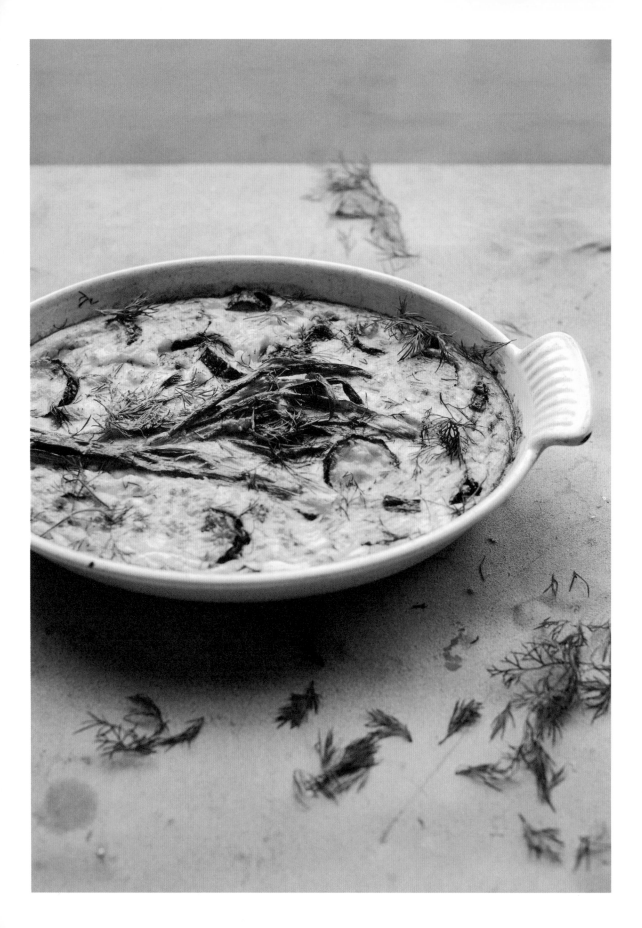

GREEK COURGETTE, POLENTA, FETA CHEESE & DILL 'PIE'

SERVES 4, OR 6–8 AS A SIDE DISH

1kg (2lb 4oz) courgettes, cut into 2cm (¾in) thick slices

3 tablespoons extra virgin olive oil

sea salt flakes and freshly ground black pepper

125g (4½oz) spring onions, trimmed

5 medium eggs, lightly beaten

150g (5½oz) Greek yogurt

35g (1¼oz) medium polenta

135g (4¾oz) feta cheese, crumbled

50g (1¾oz) kefalotyri or pecorino cheese, finely grated

20g (¾oz) dill, leaves chopped, any coarse stalks discarded, plus more to serve

3 garlic cloves, finely grated

This is based on a Greek dish which sounded very promising, but I had to cook it many times before I got a 'set' that was soft, rather than like an oven-baked frittata. It's definitely a main course dish. I often eat it just with salad.

Preheat the oven to 190°C fan (400°F), Gas Mark 6.

Put the courgettes into a large roasting tin in which they can lie – more or less – in a single layer. Toss them with 2 tablespoons of the olive oil and season. Roast for 10 minutes, then add the spring onions and trickle the remaining 1 tablespoon of oil over them. Return to the oven and roast for another 10–15 minutes. By this time, the courgettes should be tender when pierced with a sharp knife, and the spring onions slightly scorched.

Reduce the oven temperature to 170°C fan (350°F), Gas Mark 4.

In a large bowl, mix together all the other ingredients and season well. Spoon the vegetables into a gratin dish; mine measures 27 x 20 x 5cm (10½ x 8 x 2in) and has a capacity of 1 litre (1¾ pints). A cast-iron or copper dish is best, as the metals conduct heat well. Pour the batter over the vegetables and bake in the oven for 15–20 minutes, or until just set, golden and slightly souffléd. Serve hot or warm, scattered with dill.

CHILLI-ROAST TOMATOES WITH FETA CHEESE, YOGURT, DILL, MINT & PISTACHIOS

SERVES 4 AS A SIDE DISH,
OR AS PART OF A SPREAD
OF DISHES

750g (1lb 10oz) plum tomatoes, halved lengthways

4 tablespoons extra virgin olive oil

3 teaspoons chilli flakes

2 teaspoons fennel seeds

sea salt flakes and freshly ground black pepper

4 teaspoons runny honey

225g (8oz) Greek yogurt, or more, depending on the size of your serving plate

150g (5½oz) feta cheese, crumbled

1 garlic clove, finely grated

5g (⅛oz) dill, chopped, any coarse stalks removed

10g (¼oz) mint leaves

10g (¼oz) shelled unsalted pistachio nuts, chopped

Cooking is often about balance and contrast, and I particularly like dishes where the contrast is extreme. Hot, spicy tomatoes with cold, sharp yogurt is especially hard to resist. You can change the herbs here: dill, mint, chervil and coriander all work. Using chopped walnuts instead of pistachios makes quite a difference, too. It's definitely time to get out your favourite extra virgin olive oil. A Ligurian oil makes this buttery, a Greek oil a bit more robust: your choice will really change the character of the dish.

Preheat the oven to 190°C fan (400°F), Gas Mark 6.

Put all the tomatoes into a roasting tin in which they can lie in a single layer; if they are too close to each other, they will just steam instead of roasting. Spoon 3 tablespoons of the oil over them, then turn them over with your hands so they get well coated. Leave them cut sides up.

Put the chilli flakes and fennel seeds into a mortar and bash them. You won't break the fennel seeds down, but you'll crush them a bit. Sprinkle these over the tomatoes and season. Mix the honey with the remaining olive oil and spoon a little over each tomato.

Cook for 30 minutes, but keep an eye on them: you may find they need a little longer, but don't overcook them. They get to a point when they completely collapse and – even though they're delicious at this stage – they've lost all their shape and you don't want that here.

Stir the yogurt, feta and garlic together and season. Put the yogurt on a serving plate and pile the roast tomatoes on top. Sprinkle the herbs and pistachios all over the dish and serve.

ROAST RADISHES WITH HONEY, MINT & PRESERVED LEMON

SERVES 4 AS A SIDE DISH

500g (1lb 2oz) radishes, with green leaves attached

1 tablespoon extra virgin olive oil

1 tablespoon white balsamic vinegar

1 preserved lemon, flesh discarded, rind cut into shreds, plus 2 tablespoons brine from the jar, plus more if needed

10g (¼oz) unsalted butter

sea salt flakes and freshly ground black pepper

1½ tablespoons runny honey

leaves from 6 mint sprigs, torn

I used to think that roasting radishes was done just for the sake of creating something different. I couldn't see how their peppery crunch could be improved upon. But cooked radishes are just different. They retain a little of their heat – though it's muted – and they don't soften completely. They're very good with butter and a drop of lemon juice or vinegar. You need perfect radishes for this dish, crispily fresh with plenty of perky leaves.

Preheat the oven to 190°C (400°F), Gas Mark 6.

Wash the radishes well and remove their leaves (keep them fresh: you can wrap them in damp kitchen paper and put them in the fridge).

Halve the radishes lengthways. Put them in a roasting tin with the olive oil, white balsamic, half the preserved lemon brine and all the butter. Season. Roast for 7 minutes.

Add the remaining tablespoon of brine and the honey. Shake the pan around and return to the oven for a final 10 minutes.

Transfer to a warmed serving dish and mix in the reserved radish leaves; they will wilt in the heat. Stir in the shredded preserved lemon rind and taste for seasoning (you might want a little more of the brine). Scatter on the mint leaves and serve.

FROM THE OVEN

I am an inveterate roaster – it's my favourite cooking method – partly because it's lazy. You don't have to brown pieces of meat, or nudge the lid on your casserole to regulate the reduction of cooking juices. Beef caramelizes to sweetness, the skin on a chicken becomes crisp with salt and bronzed; you can sense that they will be tender. We mostly associate roasting with meat, but I like it so much as an approach that I've tried it on nearly everything. Its dry heat works on fruit, vegetables and fish, scorching the edges of peach halves and wedges of pumpkin. It intensifies flavour, which is why woolly apricots and insipid tomatoes become something else entirely, their essence – hiding in there the whole time – distilled, and their sweetness brought to the fore.

You have to learn to use your oven well; if you're cooking a main course, it makes sense to shove in a tray of peppers or tomatoes that will see you through the next few days, too. I am nearly always roasting or baking a dish to eat that night and raiding the fridge to see what else can be usefully cooked on another shelf at the same time. I even use the oven to cook steaks and pork chops (my steaks and chops are 'sear-roasted': once you've tried this, you'll find it's easier than cooking them on the hob and it produces great results).

Originally, roasting wasn't done in a closed box, but in front of a fire, the meat either on the hearth or suspended from a hook, and someone had to move it around to make sure it cooked evenly. It was the price of fuel that led to the development, during the late 18th century in England and in the American colonies, of a 'closed hearth', the precursor to the modern oven. Not everyone liked it. Some food writers decried the loss of 'proper' roasts claiming, as English writer Dorothy Hartley did, that meat cooked in this closed chamber was now baked rather than roasted. In fact, baking and roasting are both about cooking in dry heat, it's what we are cooking that usually dictates the word we use: bread is baked, chickens are roasted. Fat has a role to play in dictating which term is used as well. The difference between a roast potato and a baked one is that the first is cooked in fat.

Roasting – cooking in dry heat – is not the only thing that goes on in the oven. When you cook meat in a covered pot with a little liquid (and vegetables or aromatics), it's called pot-roasting and there are a few recipes in here for pot roasts, too. The redoubtable Anne Willan, in her *Complete Guide to Cookery*, writes that pot-roasting 'is not at all precise. It means to cook in the oven in a covered casserole but with what, and how, is up to the cook'. It can be as simple as browning a chicken, then setting it on a bed of chopped onions and herbs, adding a splash of vermouth and letting the meat make its own juices, or it can be surrounded by more liquid – stock or wine – and larger vegetables (whole waxy potatoes, carrots and leeks). The vegetables become more than just an accompaniment, as they've cooked in the meat's juices. Apart from the convenience of having meat and vegetables together – so you don't have to cook a side dish – the key thing with this approach is the moistness of the flesh and the exchange of flavours. The moist heat created in the pot produces a very different result from the dry heat of roasting.

There are also many recipes in this book that use an approach somewhere between dry roasting and pot roasting. The protein being roasted – usually chicken thighs or fish – sits on a layer of vegetables moistened with a little stock, alcohol or water. If you've salted the chicken skin, it will become crisp and you end up with a dish that is part braise, part roast: vegetables imbued with meat juices and a bit of burnished protein on top. There's no carving and the dish can be served straight from the pan. There are also recipes in which rice – long-grain rice or Spanish paella rice – is cooked in the oven in stock, the liquid becoming absorbed by the fattening grains while meat, fish or vegetables cook on top. To me, these offer the best of all possible worlds, dishes transformed by the heat of the oven that have everything: a golden finish, moist vegetables and starch.

And don't think that it's always meat that is the star. Chucking vegetables – roots or Mediterranean vegetables, wedges of cabbage or trays of purple sprouting broccoli – into the oven (once they've been tossed in melted butter or olive oil) is something I do most evenings. If the main dish doesn't include vegetables, I cook them alongside (and these days vegetables are often the main dish, not a support act). Even peas, radishes and green beans can be cooked in the oven. Roasting makes them taste even more themselves, their character concentrated rather than lost.

When roasting different vegetables together you have to be aware of their different cooking times, adding each vegetable at the right moment (green beans to roast tomatoes once the tomatoes are becoming caramelized), and you need to cut them to the correct size, too, so they can cook together and be ready at the same time. The more you cook vegetables in the oven, the more you find out what each requires.

Most of the recipes are very straightforward, but there's a couple of things to remember when you're cooking in the oven: bring the food to room temperature beforehand, and heat the oven in advance. An oven thermometer is invaluable. I use it to check the temperature both before cooking – to make sure the oven has hit the temperature to which it's set – and during cooking. Oven temperatures fluctuate. When that happens, I adjust it. I also get my oven calibrated fairly regularly. No matter how stellar your oven, there's a good chance that it's a little hotter or a little cooler than it says it is. You may try recipes in this book and find that it takes a bit longer or, perhaps, less time to get the required result. Make a note of this, so that you know what to do the next time.

Cooking food in the oven is easy, but it brings another pleasure too; although I know I'm the one who has smeared the bird with butter, mixed the crumble with my fingers or halved the peppers and turned them over in olive oil, I always feel, when I take food out of the oven, that someone else has cooked it. I've basically been drinking wine and enjoying the smell as it starts to permeate the kitchen; the cooking has done itself.

When you put meat or a pile of roasted vegetables on a platter, you don't feel that you are serving it, but that it is serving itself: it looks like an offering. This is one of the reasons I don't think cooking is difficult, or it certainly doesn't have to be. The alchemy of heat is a gift. With only a little knowledge – and gradual practice – you can learn how to use the warmth within that closed box.

BAKED PEPPERS STUFFED WITH GOAT'S CHEESE, RICOTTA & BASIL

This can be a side dish, a starter or even a main course, if it's served with another vegetable dish. The peppers are good with roast lamb and chicken, too. You can add chopped artichokes – the ones you buy in olive oil in jars – to the stuffing as well.

Preheat the oven to 180°C fan (375°F), Gas Mark 5.

Halve the peppers, deseed them, brush them with olive oil and put them into a gratin dish from which they can be served.

Drain the ricotta and the goat's cheese (there can be a little moisture lying on top of them). Mix together all 3 cheeses with seasoning, the basil, egg and garlic, gently mashing. Add the pine nuts, if you're using them.

Spoon the mixture into the pepper halves and bake for 40 minutes. The filling should be golden and souffléd and the peppers completely tender when pierced with a sharp knife. If they're not ready, return them to the oven for an extra 5–10 minutes, then test again.

6 medium peppers

a little extra virgin olive oil

150g (5½oz) ricotta (fresh rather than UHT, if possible)

300g (10½oz) soft goat's cheese

50g (1¾oz) Parmesan cheese, finely grated

sea salt flakes and freshly ground black pepper

30g (1oz) basil leaves, torn

1 medium egg

1 garlic clove, crushed

15g (½oz) toasted pine nuts (optional)

MOROCCAN ROAST VEGETABLES WITH LABNEH

If you don't want to serve the labneh – though it's only drained yogurt that you leave in the fridge overnight to make itself – then just stir a couple of chopped preserved lemons into a bowl of Greek yogurt and offer that alongside the vegetables instead.

Start the labneh the day before. Put the yogurt into a piece of muslin or a brand new all-purpose kitchen cloth set in a sieve over a bowl. Stir in some salt and pepper. Pull the fabric up round the yogurt to make a 'bag'. Put the whole thing – including the bowl to catch the moisture that drains out – in the fridge for 24 hours. Give it a gentle squeeze every so often. You'll get a firm yogurt 'cheese'.

Preheat the oven to 190°C (400°F), Gas Mark 6.

Cut the squash into wedges (I don't peel it, as the skin softens enough during roasting to be edible) and remove the seeds. Divide between 2 roasting tins, then do the same with the onions, cauliflower and potatoes. The vegetables need to be able to lie in a single layer, with room to add the tomatoes later. Season, add the chillies, ginger, cumin and harissa and drizzle everything with 5 tablespoons of the olive oil. Turn the vegetables, so they get covered in the flavourings and oil. Roast for 20 minutes.

Stir in the chickpeas and garlic, add the tomato bunches and drizzle with the rest of the olive oil. Roast for a final 20 minutes, or until the vegetables are tender and slightly singed in places. Check the seasoning.

Transfer the vegetables to a warmed platter or shallow bowl. Squeeze over the lemon juice and scatter with the coriander and shredded preserved lemon rind. Serve the vegetables and labneh on their own – the dish already contains a starch in the potatoes – or with couscous.

SERVES 6

FOR THE LABNEH

150g (5½oz) Greek yogurt

sea salt flakes and freshly ground black pepper

FOR THE VEGETABLES

2kg (4lb 8oz) squash or pumpkin (Crown Prince has a good flavour)

3 onions, cut into thick wedges

1 medium cauliflower, broken into florets

400g (14oz) baby potatoes, scrubbed and quartered

2–3 red chillies, halved, deseeded and finely sliced

3cm (1¼in) fresh root ginger, peeled and finely grated

½ tablespoon ground cumin

1 tablespoon harissa

7 tablespoons extra virgin olive oil

2 x 400g cans of chickpeas, drained and rinsed

4 garlic cloves, finely sliced

200g (7oz) cherry tomatoes on the vine, snipped into small bunches

juice of ½ lemon

leaves from a small bunch of coriander, chopped, to serve

3 preserved lemons, rind only, shredded, to serve

couscous, to serve (optional)

OREGANO-ROAST AUBERGINES WITH ANCHOVY & CHILLI SAUCE

Aubergines roast to a lovely velvety softness and can take any flavours you care to throw at them. Despite their subtlety, they seem to be able to hold their own. This anchovy sauce is simple and is also excellent with roast tomatoes and roast peppers: salty with sweet.

Preheat the oven to 190°C fan (400°F), Gas Mark 6.

Halve the aubergines and cut a cross-hatched pattern in the flesh of each one, without cutting right the way through to the skin (this helps the heat to penetrate better). Put these on to a rimmed baking sheet – line it with baking parchment or foil if you want – and smear the olive oil evenly all over the cut surfaces. Toss in the oregano, too, and salt and pepper. Turn the aubergines over with your hands, making sure the seasoning and some of the herb leaves go into the flesh.

Roast, cut side up, for about 40 minutes, or until the aubergines are tender right through and golden. Squeeze the lemon juice over the top.

To make the sauce, pound the rosemary and garlic in a mortar, then add the anchovies and crush to a paste. Gradually add the lemon juice and then the olive oil, a little at a time, grinding as you go. You aren't making a mayonnaise – so don't expect this to emulsify, you'll be left with a lumpy 'sauce' – but the pounding melds all the elements together. Add the chilli and set aside. The longer the sauce sits with the chilli, the hotter it will become.

Serve the aubergines with the sauce, either on the side or spooned over the top. You need good bread with this, to mop up all the juices.

SERVES 4 AS A SIDE DISH

FOR THE AUBERGINES

4 medium-large aubergines

4 tablespoons extra virgin olive oil

leaves from 3 oregano sprigs, torn

sea salt flakes and freshly ground black pepper

juice of ½ lemon

good crusty bread, to serve

FOR THE SAUCE

leaves from 2 rosemary sprigs

2 garlic cloves, chopped

14 anchovies, drained of oil

juice of 1 lemon, or to taste

4 tablespoons extra virgin olive oil

1 red chilli, halved, deseeded and chopped, plus more if you want it hotter

BAKED FENNEL WITH CHILLI & PARMESAN CHEESE

SERVES 6–8 AS
A SIDE DISH

4 fennel bulbs

3 tablespoons extra virgin olive oil

2 garlic cloves, finely grated

3 teaspoons fennel seeds, coarsely crushed in a mortar

3 teaspoons chilli flakes

sea salt flakes and freshly ground black pepper

25g (scant 1oz) Parmesan cheese, finely grated

I used to blanch fennel before roasting it, but if the oven is really hot, you don't need to. This is one of my favourite side dishes. I could eat it by the plateful. To make it into a main course, serve it with burrata, your favourite extra virgin olive oil and warm focaccia. As a side dish, it works well with roast lamb, chicken and fish.

Preheat the oven to 190°C fan (400°F), Gas Mark 6.

Trim the tips of the fennel bulbs, halve the bulbs and remove any coarse or discoloured outer leaves (reserve any little fronds you find). Cut each half into 2–2.5cm (¾–1in) thick wedges, keeping them intact at the base. Toss in a bowl with the olive oil, garlic, fennel seeds, chilli flakes, any reserved fennel fronds and plenty of seasoning. Put into a gratin dish and cover tightly with foil.

Bake for about 20 minutes (the undersides should turn pale gold), then remove the foil, sprinkle on the Parmesan and return to the oven for a final 10–15 minutes, or until the fennel is tender (check it by piercing a piece with a sharp knife) and the top is golden.

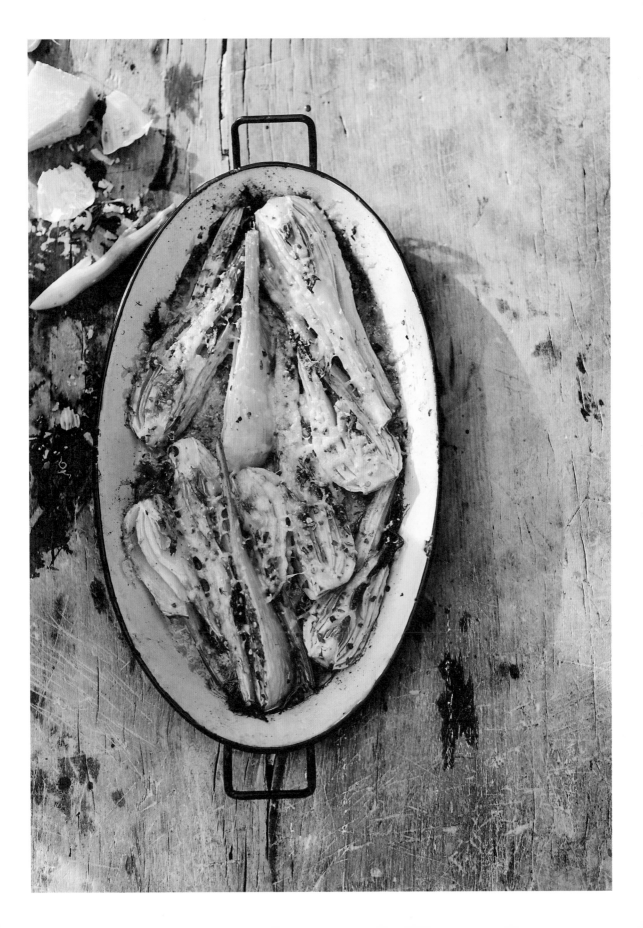

BUTTER-ROAST AUBERGINES & TOMATOES WITH FREEKEH & KOCH-KOCHA

More buttery aubergines... and what a revelation this dish is. There's nothing to it, it's just aubergines and tomatoes roasted with garlicky butter, but it tastes more complex than you would expect. The cooked freekeh becomes lovely and sticky round the edges as it bakes in the vegetable juices, too. Koch-kocha is an Ethiopian sauce, a bit like Yemeni zhug. You don't need to get grains of paradise or ajwain for it (some bashed caraway seeds will do instead of the ajwain and grains of paradise are peppery and coriander-like, so substitute toasted and crushed coriander seeds). You can buy both online, though. I've used oil in the sauce, but you can just use water.

Preheat the oven to 190°C fan (400°F), Gas Mark 6.

Pierce each aubergine with the tip of a knife – you don't have to remove the tops – and cut the tomatoes in half. Put them into a roasting tin or a shallow casserole 30cm (12in) in diameter; they don't have to *quite* lie in a single layer but they should almost do so.

Melt the butter in a saucepan and add the garlic. Cook over a low heat for a few minutes, then pour the butter all over the vegetables, turning them over. Season and sprinkle each tomato half with a little sugar if they aren't very sweet; if you have great tomatoes you won't need it.

Roast for 30 minutes, turning the aubergines over once during this time.

For the koch-kocha sauce, simply put everything into a food processor and whizz until smooth.

Add the freekeh to the roasting tin, pushing it down under the vegetables (you don't want it sprinkled on top of them). Return to the oven for a final 5–10 minutes, or until the tomatoes are caramelized, the aubergines are tender right through and the freekeh has become slightly sticky at the edges. Serve the dish with the sauce, a big bowl of natural yogurt and good bread.

SERVES 4

FOR THE VEGETABLES AND FREEKEH

1kg (2lb 4oz) baby aubergines

1kg (2lb 4oz) plum tomatoes (you can use a mixture of colours – red, green and yellow – as long as they are about the same size)

100g (3½oz) unsalted butter

12 garlic cloves, not too finely sliced

sea salt flakes and freshly ground black pepper

a little soft light brown sugar (optional, only if your tomatoes aren't sweet)

250g (9oz) cooked freekeh

natural yogurt, to serve

good bread, to serve

FOR THE KOCH-KOCHA

½ green pepper, halved, deseeded and roughly chopped

50g (1¾oz) coriander leaves

1 red chilli and 1 green chilli, halved and deseeded

3cm (1¼in) fresh root ginger, peeled and finely grated

juice of 1 lime

½ tablespoon cider vinegar, or white wine vinegar

1 garlic clove, finely grated

1 teaspoon ground cumin

1 teaspoon ground cardamom seeds

¼ teaspoon crushed grains of paradise

½ teaspoon crushed ajwain

100ml (3½fl oz) extra virgin olive oil

ROAST AUBERGINE PURÉE WITH GOAT'S CURD, SMOKED ALMONDS, CHILLI & ROSEMARY

SERVES 6 AS A SIDE DISH

3 aubergines

5 tablespoons extra virgin olive oil

2 teaspoons harissa

sea salt flakes and freshly ground black pepper

2 garlic cloves (not too large), finely grated

juice of ½ lemon, or to taste

100g (3½oz) goat's curd or creamy goat's cheese

10g (¼oz) smoked almonds, roughly chopped (you want quite big bits)

2 red chillies, halved, deseeded and very finely sliced

leaves from 1 rosemary sprig, chopped

warm flatbread or toasted sourdough bread, to serve

Another dish that shows off the soft, collapsing flesh of roast aubergines. You could finish this purée in other ways: with feta cheese, melted butter and chopped dill, or with capers tossed in a vinaigrette with chopped anchovies and olives.

Preheat the oven to 190°C fan (400°F), Gas Mark 6.

Put the aubergines in a roasting tin and brush lightly with some of the olive oil. Pierce each a few times with the tines of a fork. Roast for 40–45 minutes, or until the aubergines are completely soft and look a bit deflated.

Leave until cool enough to handle, then slit the skins and scoop the flesh out into a bowl. Chop the flesh (it will be totally soft, you just need to break it down a bit), mash and add about 3½ tablespoons of the oil, the harissa, salt, pepper, garlic and lemon juice to taste. Put this into a warmed serving bowl and scatter the goat's curd or cheese on top.

Heat the remaining extra virgin olive oil in a frying pan and quickly fry the smoked almonds, chillies and rosemary together (you just want to take the rawness off the chillies a little). Pour this over the roast aubergines and serve with bread.

SMOKED PAPRIKA-BAKED COURGETTES, TOMATOES & GREEN BEANS WITH EGGS

This is a blueprint for baked eggs and vegetables. The flavours here are quite Spanish (you can also add sautéed chorizo to the dish), but you can make a completely different version by leaving out the smoked paprika and adding slices of Parma ham and grated Parmesan or pecorino cheese along with the eggs.

Preheat the oven to 190°C fan (400°F), Gas Mark 6.

Trim the ends from the courgettes and cut them into 5mm (¼in) thick slices. Put all the vegetables except the green beans into a shallow casserole, ideally about 30cm (12in) across, or a roasting tin in which they can all lie in a single layer. Add 2 tablespoons of the olive oil, the seasoning, thyme, chilli (if you want heat), smoked paprika and garlic. Toss everything together and bake for 30 minutes, turning the vegetables over a couple of times.

Toss the green beans with the remaining oil and scatter them on top of the other vegetables. Return to the oven for 8 minutes.

Break the eggs on top, season and return the casserole or tin to the oven for a final 8 minutes or so. The eggs should be cooked.

Serve straight from the pan, sprinkling the eggs with a little more paprika, if you like. If you've made it very spicy – and I often do – a bowl of Greek yogurt on the side is good.

SERVES 4

4 courgettes

400g (14oz) small waxy potatoes, scrubbed and quartered

330g (11½oz) cherry tomatoes

12 spring onions, trimmed

3 tablespoons extra virgin olive oil

sea salt flakes and freshly ground black pepper

leaves from 3 thyme sprigs, plus 5 whole thyme sprigs

½ teaspoon chilli flakes (optional)

¾ tablespoon smoked paprika, plus more to serve

4 garlic cloves, finely grated

250g (9oz) green beans, topped but not tailed

6–8 large eggs

Greek yogurt, to serve (optional)

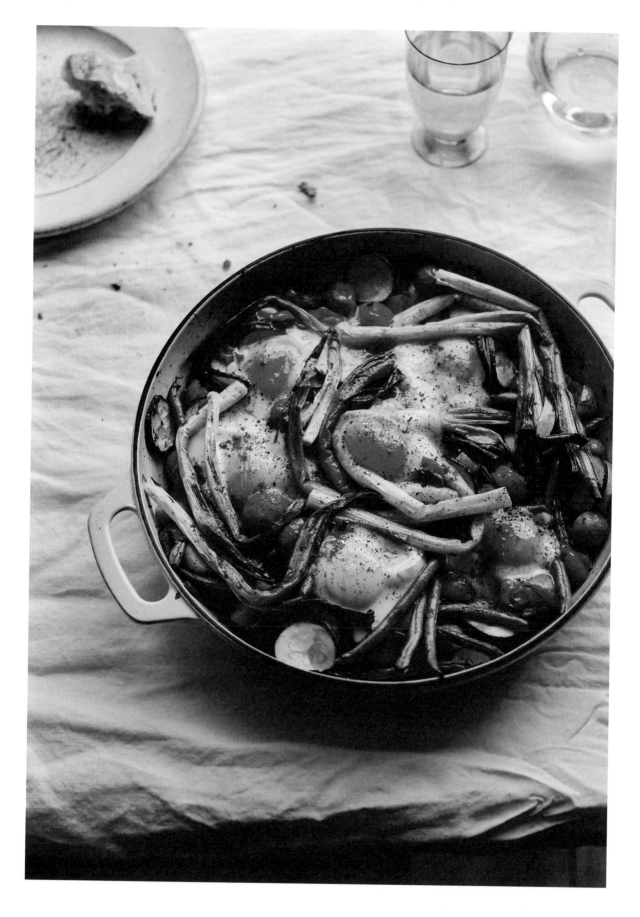

ROAST ASPARAGUS WITH RICOTTA & PECORINO CHEESE

SERVES 4 AS A STARTER, OR AS PART OF A SPREAD OF DISHES

300g (10½oz) asparagus spears, of medium thickness

extra virgin olive oil

sea salt flakes and freshly ground black pepper

125g (4½oz) ricotta cheese (fresh rather than UHT, if possible)

pecorino cheese, or Parmesan cheese, shaved

The simplest of dishes and without the hassle of trying (and failing) to prop your asparagus spears up against the side of a saucepan. The stalks should ideally be about the same thickness, so that they're all ready at the same time. If you get good fresh ricotta – not UHT stuff – this is food fit for the gods.

Preheat the oven to 210°C fan (425°F), Gas Mark 7.

Trim the woody ends from the asparagus spears, put them on an ovenproof tray with a slight lip and drizzle with olive oil. Season with salt.

Roast for 10–12 minutes, or until the asparagus spears are tender (test one of the thickest with the tip of a sharp knife).

Put the asparagus on to a serving plate. Scatter the ricotta in nuggets over the top, followed by the shaved pecorino or Parmesan cheese. Add salt and pepper, pour on more olive oil and serve immediately.

TOMATO, GOAT'S CHEESE & OLIVE CLAFOUTIS WITH BASIL

I'd only ever made sweet clafoutis until I thought about baking this dish and then, suddenly, it seemed obvious. It's a bit like a quiche without the pastry, only softer because it doesn't have to hold its shape in quite the same way as a tart filling. You might think this is light – and it is – but it's also deceptively rich and filling. I don't serve anything with it except some good bread.

Preheat the oven to 190°C fan (400°F), Gas Mark 6.

Put the tomatoes into a gratin dish with the olive oil and season them. Turn them over so that the surfaces are all coated in a little oil. Roast for 20–30 minutes, or until the tomatoes are soft and slightly shrunken. Take out of the oven and leave to sit on a work surface.

Reduce the oven temperature to 180°C fan (375°F), Gas Mark 5.

Put the eggs, egg yolks, flour, milk and cream into a food processor, season well and whizz. Stir in the Parmesan and garlic.

Scatter the olives over the tomatoes and crumble on the goat's cheese.

Pour the batter over the tomatoes, olives and cheese and bake for 30 minutes, until the custard is puffed, golden and just set in the middle. Leave it for 5 minutes to settle: it will sink a little once it has sat for a while. Scatter over the basil and serve.

400g (14oz) mixed cherry and plum tomatoes, halved or quartered, depending on size

1½ tablespoons extra virgin olive oil

sea salt flakes and freshly ground black pepper

4 medium eggs, plus 2 medium egg yolks

50g (1¾oz) plain flour

200ml (7fl oz) whole milk

300ml (½ pint) double cream

30g (1oz) Parmesan cheese, finely grated

1 garlic clove, finely grated

30g (1oz) pitted black olives, chopped

200g (7oz) goat's cheese, crumbled

10g (¼oz) basil leaves, torn

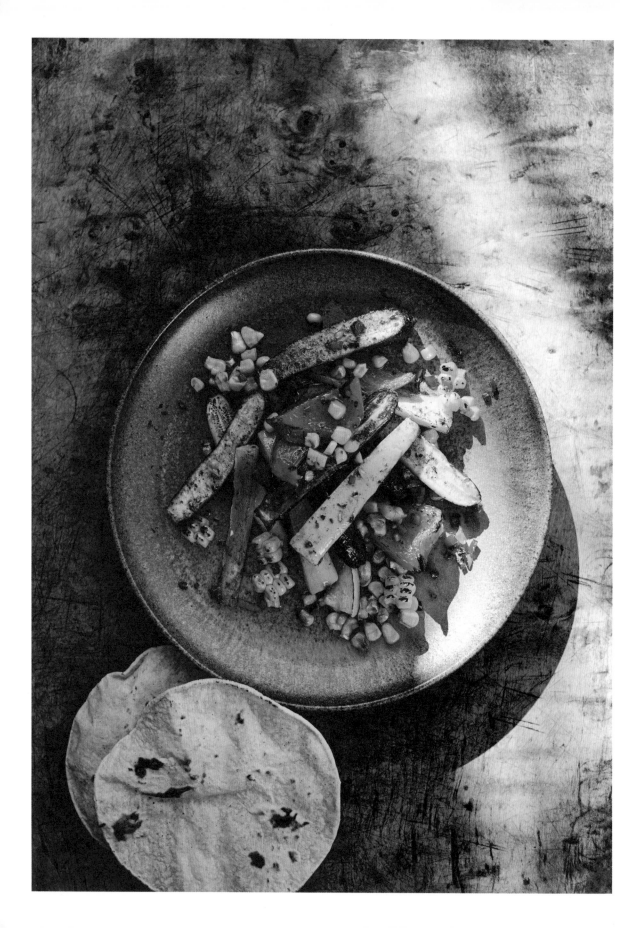

ROAST CORN, COURGETTES & PEPPERS WITH CUMIN, CHILLI, SOURED CREAM & AVOCADO

SERVES 4 WITH
SOMETHING STARCHY
ON THE SIDE, OR 6–8
AS A SIDE DISH

FOR THE VEGETABLES

4 ears of sweetcorn

5 courgettes, cut into chunky batons

2 red peppers, halved, deseeded and cut into broad strips

1 green and 2 red chillies, halved, deseeded and very finely sliced

3 teaspoons ground cumin

¾ teaspoon ground cinnamon

2 teaspoons dried oregano (preferably Mexican oregano, but regular will do)

4 garlic cloves, finely grated

4 tablespoons extra virgin olive oil

sea salt flakes and freshly ground black pepper

5g (⅛oz) coriander leaves

TO SERVE

2 avocados

juice of 1 lime, plus lime wedges to serve

200g (7oz) soured cream

100g (3½oz) cheese, such as Lancashire, Wensleydale or feta, crumbled

rice, quinoa or tortillas

I love roast corn. Before I first cooked it this way, I couldn't see the point of it, but now it's the only type of corn I want. Roasting condenses its sweetness, but it also gives it a toasted 'popcorn' flavour. If you can get slim young courgettes you only need to halve them lengthways, you don't have to cut them into batons, but they vary a lot throughout the season and you probably won't have much choice in what you buy. It's important to roast the corn on its own, not with the other vegetables, otherwise the moisture in the courgettes and peppers won't allow the corn to toast properly. Serve with warm corn or wheat tortillas, rice or quinoa.

Preheat the oven to 190°C fan (400°F), Gas Mark 6.

Hold an ear of corn standing up in a roasting tin. Using a sharp knife, cut down the sides, removing the kernels as you work round. (Try to keep some in strips; cut close to the core to achieve this.) Repeat with the other ears.

Put the courgettes and peppers into another roasting tin. In a small bowl, mix together the chillies, spices, oregano, garlic, olive oil and seasoning. Mix two-thirds of this with the courgettes and peppers (reserve the rest of the mixture), tossing with your hands so that all the vegetables get coated.

Roast the courgettes and peppers in the oven for 20 minutes, then turn them over. Toss the rest of the oil and spices with the corn, season and roast that, in its separate tin, alongside the other vegetables for a final 20 minutes.

Halve and pit the avocados. Squeeze lime juice all over the surfaces and season. Serve the roasted vegetables in a warmed broad shallow bowl, scattered with the coriander leaves, along with the halved avocados – people can help themselves to the flesh – the soured cream, cheese and lime wedges. Offer rice, quinoa or tortillas on the side.

SERVES 4 AS A STARTER

6 red peppers

a little extra virgin olive oil

sea salt flakes and freshly
ground black pepper

60g (2¼oz) 'nduja

about 400g (14oz) burrata

ciabatta, to serve

ROAST PEPPERS WITH BURRATA & 'NDUJA

You barely need a recipe for this, it's just distinctive ingredients, melting together, each providing a contrast to its neighbour: chilli-hot 'nduja that falls apart in the heat of the oven, cold creamy burrata, and charred peppers. Most people, when you give them a plate of this and some ciabatta to mop up the juices, will just be quiet and eat.

Preheat the oven to 190°C fan (400°F), Gas Mark 6.

Halve the peppers, deseed them and put them into a gratin dish, roasting tin or a baking sheet with a lip around it. Brush them with olive oil, season and roast for 20 minutes.

Break the 'nduja into chunks and divide it among the peppers, putting it inside them. Roast for a final 10 minutes.

When they're cooked, the pepper skins should be slightly blistered and a little charred in places. Leave them until they're cool enough to handle, then tear them or leave them whole – whichever you prefer – and divide them between 4 plates. Drain the burrata, tear it and serve it alongside the peppers and 'nduja. Offer some ciabatta on the side.

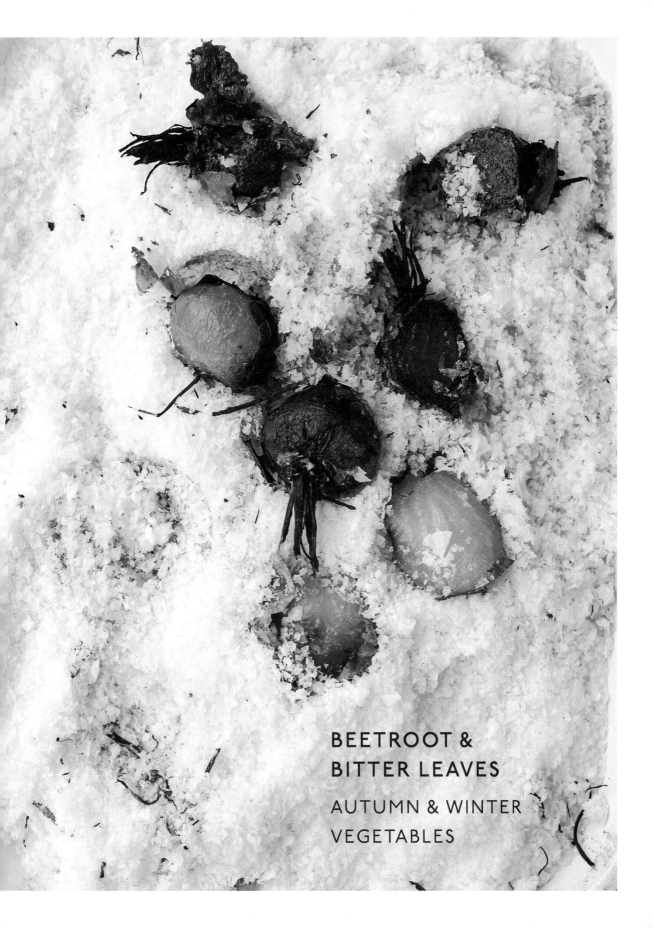

BEETROOT &
BITTER LEAVES

AUTUMN & WINTER
VEGETABLES

ROAST AUTUMN VEGETABLES WITH WALNUT-MISO SAUCE

The sauce here is rather like a vegetarian version of the Piedmontese anchovy sauce, bagna cauda *(though it's even more umami-packed). It's not one of those vegetable recipes that feels like a side dish, where you keep searching for the focus, but has enough different flavours and textures from each vegetable to be layered and surprising.*

SERVES 4

FOR THE VEGETABLES

10 slim carrots (those you buy in a bunch with greenery attached are best), in mixed colours if possible

500g (1lb 2oz) celeriac

500g (1lb 2oz) butternut squash or pumpkin, deseeded and cut into wedges about 3cm (1¼in) thick

3 large white or red onions, cut into wedges

4 tablespoons extra virgin olive oil

sea salt flakes and freshly ground black pepper

3 heads of chicory, red or white (or a mixture)

FOR THE SAUCE

55g (2oz) walnut pieces

350ml (12fl oz) extra virgin olive oil (a fruity rather than a grassy one)

75g (2¾oz) red miso paste

½ teaspoon chilli flakes

3 fat garlic cloves, finely grated

Preheat the oven to 190°C fan (400°F), Gas Mark 6.

Trim the carrots at the top and tips (if there are long straggly bits on the tips). Leave the green tufts if there are any, but wash them really well. If you haven't been able to get slim carrots, then halve them along their length.

Peel the celeriac and cut it into wedges about 1.5cm (¾in) thick. Put all the vegetables – except the chicory – into a couple of roasting tins, or baking trays that have a lip all the way around, in which they can lie in a single layer. Add the olive oil, season (don't use too much salt, as the sauce will be salty) and toss everything around with your hands.

Roast for 40 minutes, until tender and slightly scorched, turning them once. Quarter the chicory heads and add halfway through, tossing them in the oil.

Make the sauce. Pound the walnuts in a mortar – or pulse-blend in a food processor – until you have a mixture that is part finely ground and part chunky.

Pour the olive oil into a saucepan set over a very gentle heat. Add the miso and whisk it together: the miso will stay in little globules separate from the oil, but that's normal. Add the chilli and garlic and simmer very gently for about 5 minutes, stirring every so often. The garlic must not colour. Stir in the walnuts and cook for another 2 minutes.

Transfer the vegetables to a warmed platter. Either spoon the sauce over the top, or serve it on the side.

MELTING BAKED ONIONS WITH
PARMESAN CHEESE & CREAM

SERVES 6 AS A SIDE DISH,
OR AS PART OF A SPREAD
OF DISHES

6 onions, about 175g
(6oz) each

75g (2¾oz) unsalted butter

sea salt flakes and freshly
ground black pepper

4 tablespoons extra virgin
olive oil

handful of thyme sprigs

200g tub of crème fraîche

50g (1¾oz) Parmesan
cheese, finely grated

*Eating these is like having your own little bowl of cheesy onion
soup. Don't try to hurry them, they need to cook slowly. You could
use Gruyère instead of Parmesan, or go more Eastern European
and drizzle on butter in which you've sautéed caraway seeds or
paprika and serve with nuggets of bacon, or Quark or soured
cream, and smoked grated cheese. There are loads of possibilities,
but the onions are sweet, so they do need something salty. Offer as
a side dish for meat (something plain like roast chicken is best),
or serve them as a main course with another vegetable dish.*

Preheat the oven to 160°C fan (340°F), Gas Mark 3½.

Remove the outer skins of the onions, but leave on at least 1 layer of papery
skin. Trim the bases a little so that they can sit upright in the oven.

Rub some butter over the base of each onion and season the exposed flesh.
Set them in a double-thick layer of foil or baking parchment (big enough to
come up round the onions and be twisted to seal later). Pour a little olive oil
on each onion and add a few thyme sprigs. Seal the parcel and transfer to a
roasting tin.

Bake for 1¼ hours. The inside of the onions should be completely soft by
now, with juices all round the base. Open the package, split each onion open,
season, spoon some of the cooking juices inside and add a spoonful of crème
fraîche and some cheese.

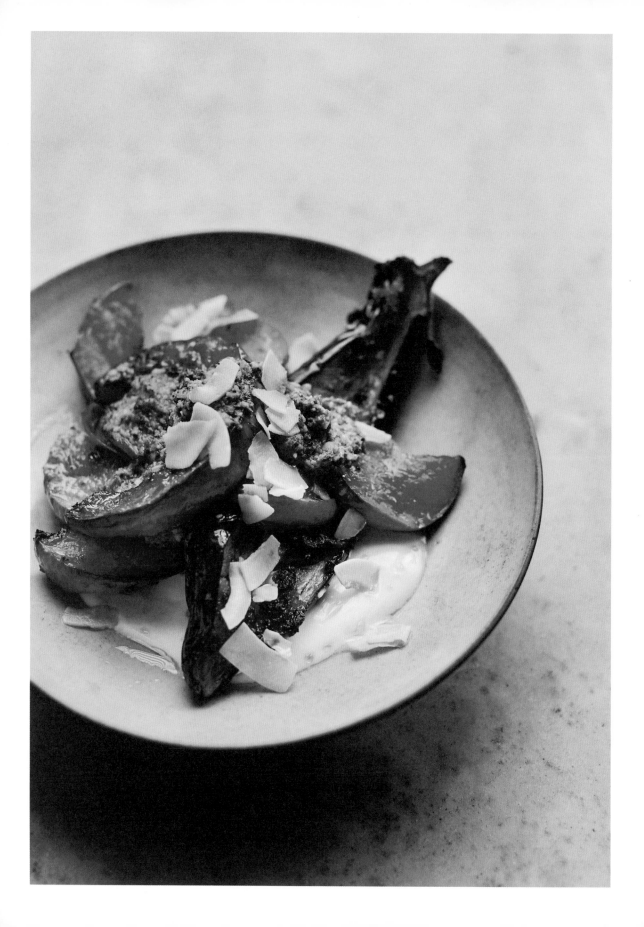

ROAST SPICED AUBERGINES, PUMPKIN & TOMATOES WITH COCONUT & GREEN CHUTNEY

This dish can be simple or slightly more complicated. The spice paste has warmth from the ginger and heat from the chilli and it's hard to believe the effect it has on the vegetables: you really can just eat them with a bowl of yogurt. But make the chutney too and you have a feast (it's also great with white and oily fish or with chicken, either on the side or stuffed under the chicken skin before roasting). The chutney can be completely savoury or slightly sweet, depending on what you want to serve it with.

Preheat the oven to 190°C fan (400°F), Gas Mark 6.

Put everything for the spice paste into a food processor and whizz. Scrape into a bowl (don't clean the food processor yet).

Halve the tomatoes and put them in a roasting tin in which they can lie in a single layer. Spoon some of the spice paste on top of each, then turn them to make sure they get well coated all over, arranging them so they're all cut side up. Halve the aubergines lengthways and cut a cross-hatched pattern in the flesh side, without cutting all the way through (this helps the heat to penetrate). Put them in a large roasting tin, which has enough room for the pumpkin to fit in later in a single layer and rub them with half the remaining spice paste, ending cut sides up. Roast both trays for 20 minutes.

Deseed the pumpkin and cut into slices – there's no need to peel them, as the skin softens while they're in the oven – about 2.5cm (1in) thick at their thickest part. Rub over the rest of the spice paste. If the mixture doesn't go quite far enough (though it should), add a little more olive oil. Add the pumpkin slices to the aubergine tin.

Return the pumpkin and aubergine tin to the oven and roast for 20 minutes, turning the pumpkin slices over halfway through this time. The vegetables

FOR THE SPICE PASTE

4cm (1½in) fresh root ginger, peeled and chopped

10 garlic cloves, chopped

3 red chillies, halved, deseeded and chopped

1 long shallot, roughly chopped

seeds from 10 cardamom pods

sea salt flakes and freshly ground black pepper

4 teaspoons soft light brown sugar

juice of 2 limes

100ml (3½fl oz) extra virgin olive oil, plus more if needed

FOR THE VEGETABLES

8 plum tomatoes

4 medium-large aubergines

900g (2lb) pumpkin or squash (Crown Prince is a well-flavoured variety)

coriander leaves, to serve (optional)

15g (½oz) unsweetened coconut flakes, toasted

natural yogurt and warmed naan bread, to serve

continued >

should now be ready – tender and golden – but keep an eye on the tomatoes so that they don't overcook (they may only take 30 minutes cooking time in total, so check on them when you turn the pumpkin slices). They should still hold their shape, not completely collapse.

To make the chutney, put everything for it in the food processor (you don't need to wash the bowl after the spice paste) and pour in 100ml (3½fl oz) water. Whizz. If you want the chutney to be a little sweet, add the sugar. Taste for seasoning and sharpness, then scrape into a bowl.

Put all the vegetables on a warmed platter and scatter over the coriander leaves with the toasted coconut.

Serve with the chutney and a bowl of yogurt (regular yogurt, for its sourness, rather than the Greek variety) and warmed naan bread.

FOR THE CHUTNEY

1 teaspoon ground cumin

50g (1¾oz) coriander, any coarse stalks removed

15g (½oz) mint leaves

25g (scant 1oz) baby spinach

100g (3½oz) creamed coconut, from a block, crumbled or coarsely grated

1 green chilli, halved, deseeded and chopped

3 garlic cloves, chopped

2.5cm (1in) fresh root ginger, peeled and chopped

finely grated zest of 1 lime and juice of 3 limes, or to taste

sea salt, to taste

1 teaspoon caster sugar, if you want a sweet version

AN OVEN FULL OF POTATOES...

As with the novel, the demise of the potato is much discussed but never actually materializes, at least not in my house. This is not an exhaustive list, but it should help you cook potatoes that will go with Mediterranean dishes, Eastern European food, Indian, Greek, or sort-of-French recipes. You can stick them in the oven on the shelf below (or alongside) whatever starchless main course you're cooking. The first dish is the most basic and can take endless simple variations. You do have to make sure your potatoes are cut to the correct (and roughly the same) size, though these are forgiving rather than exacting dishes: cooked potatoes are tender and the tip of a knife will tell you whether they're ready or not.

ROSEMARY, GARLIC & OLIVE OIL-ROAST POTATOES

The most basic bung-it-in-the-oven potatoes. I make this all the time, though sometimes leave out the garlic. Take 700g (1lb 9oz) of potatoes – waxy or floury, though they will give you different results (I usually go for waxy) – and cut them into chunks just a little smaller than a walnut. Separate the cloves from 2 heads of garlic, but don't peel them. Strip the leaves from 2 rosemary sprigs (have another 3 whole sprigs). Put all of this in a roasting tin in which everything can lie in a single layer and add 2–3 tablespoons of extra virgin olive oil, 1 tablespoon of balsamic vinegar, salt and pepper. Roast in an oven preheated to 190°C fan (400°F), Gas Mark 6 for 35 minutes, tossing them around a couple of times as they cook. Smoked paprika or chilli flakes (or both) are a good addition. SERVES 4

THYME-ROAST POTATOES WITH ONIONS, BLACK OLIVES & GOAT'S CHEESE

Halve or quarter 650g (1lb 7oz) of baby waxy potatoes. Toss them in a roasting tin in which they can lie in a single layer, with 2 red onions, cut into wedges, 3 tablespoons of extra virgin olive oil, 1 tablespoon of balsamic vinegar, salt, pepper and 8 thyme sprigs. Roast in an oven preheated to 190°C fan (400°F), Gas Mark 6 for 35 minutes, shaking halfway through. About 7 minutes before the end of cooking time, add 30g (1oz) of small black olives (unpitted are fine) and 150g (5½oz) of goat's cheese, broken into chunks. SERVES 4

ROAST POTATOES WITH FETA CHEESE, GREEN CHILLIES & MINT

Halve or quarter 700g (1lb 9oz) of baby waxy potatoes. Put them in a roasting tin in which they can lie in a single layer, toss in 3 tablespoons of extra virgin olive oil and season. Put them in an oven preheated to 190°C fan (400°F), Gas Mark 6 and cook for 20 minutes. Take them out and add 1–2 green chillies – depending on how hot you want the dish to be – halved, deseeded and finely shredded. Toss everything around in the oil and return to the oven for a final 15–20 minutes. Add 50g (1¾oz) of crumbled feta cheese and the torn leaves from 6 mint sprigs. Squeeze lemon or lime juice over the top and serve. SERVES 4

ROAST POTATOES WITH BACON, SPRING ONIONS, PAPRIKA & CARAWAY

Halve or quarter 650g (1lb 7oz) of baby waxy potatoes. Put them in a roasting tin in which they can lie in a single layer and add 1 large onion, cut into wedges about 1cm (½in) thick, 200g (7oz) of chunky bacon lardons (they really must be quite big), 2 teaspoons of caraway seeds, 2 teaspoons of sweet paprika and 2 tablespoons of extra virgin olive oil. Toss everything round and roast for 20 minutes in an oven preheated to 190°C fan (400°F), Gas Mark 6, then brush a little oil on 150g (5½oz) of trimmed spring onions. Toss the vegetables and bacon, lay the spring onions on top and roast for 15 minutes. The potatoes should be tender and the spring onions soft and a little scorched. SERVES 4–6

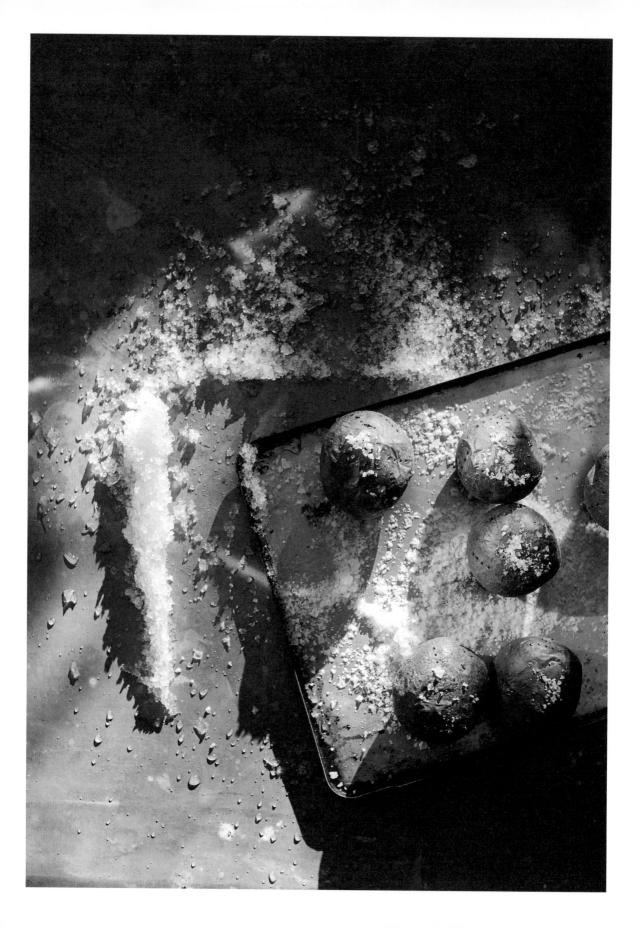

ROAST POTATOES & TOMATOES WITH ANCHOVIES, CAPERS, FENNEL & ROSEMARY

Halve or quarter 650g (1lb 7oz) of baby waxy potatoes. Put them in a roasting tin in which they can lie in a single layer and toss them with 2 tablespoons of extra virgin olive oil, the roughly chopped leaves of 2 rosemary sprigs, ¼–½ teaspoon of chilli flakes and ¼ teaspoon of fennel seeds (bash the fennel a little in a mortar first). Roast in an oven preheated to 190°C fan (400°F), Gas Mark 6 for 15 minutes, then add 300g (10½oz) of cherry tomatoes. Toss them round and roast for another 15 minutes. Add 10 chopped anchovies from a jar, plus 1 tablespoon of their oil, and 2 tablespoons of rinsed and drained capers, patted dry. Toss everything around again and return to the oven for a final 5 minutes. Taste. The capers and anchovies are salty, so you shouldn't need seasoning. SERVES 4

BABY POTATOES & LEEKS BAKED IN PAPER WITH HERB BUTTER

Mash 35g (1¼oz) of unsalted butter with 2 tablespoons of mixed finely chopped chives and flat leaf parsley leaves (chervil is good, too, if you can get it) and a splash of dry white vermouth. Halve or quarter 500g (1lb 2oz) of baby waxy potatoes. Trim 2 leeks, discard the coarse outer leaves and cut into lengths of about 3cm (1¼in). Cut out 6 rectangles of baking parchment, each about 36 x 30cm (14 x 12in). Put the potatoes, leeks and seasoning in the middle of each piece of paper and add a generous knob of the butter. Bring the edges of the paper together and roll them tightly, allowing some room around the potatoes, then twist the ends to seal. Put on a baking sheet and bake for 35–40 minutes in an oven preheated to 200°C fan (410°F), Gas Mark 6½. The packages will puff up and the vegetables should be tender. Serve them in the parcels, so people can open them at the table. SERVES 6

INDIAN-SPICED ROAST POTATOES & CAULIFLOWER

A kind of roasted aloo gobi. Cut 500g (1lb 2oz) of floury potatoes into chunks the size of a walnut (peel them if you have time) and break a small cauliflower into florets (keep the leaves). Toss the potatoes and cauliflower florets (reserve the leaves) in a bowl with 4 chopped plum tomatoes, 3 teaspoons of cumin seeds and 1 teaspoon of coriander seeds (toasted in a dry pan for a minute, then crushed a bit). Add 1 teaspoon of chilli powder (preferably mild red Kashmiri), 1 teaspoon of ground turmeric and 35g (1¼oz) of fresh root ginger, peeled and finely grated. Add 4 tablespoons of groundnut oil, salt and pepper and toss with your hands. Spread out in a large roasting tin or oven tray (use 2 if you need to) in which everything can lie in a single layer. Roast in an oven preheated to 200°C fan (410°F), Gas Mark 6½ for 20 minutes, turning every so often. Add 2 garlic cloves, finely grated, and the cauliflower leaves, toss and roast for a final 10 minutes. The vegetables should be tender and golden. Sprinkle with chopped coriander leaves and lime juice. SERVES 4–6

ROAST SWEET POTATOES WITH CAYENNE & SPINACH

Wash 3 medium-small sweet potatoes, remove any little tufts from the surface and cut into 2–3cm (1in) chunks. Toss in a bowl with 2 tablespoons of extra virgin olive oil and 1 teaspoon of cayenne pepper, salt and pepper. Transfer to a large, shallow baking tray and put into the top of an oven preheated to 200°C fan (410°F), Gas Mark 6½. Roast for 50 minutes, turning once during cooking. Stir in a couple of handfuls of torn spinach leaves – they wilt in the heat of the potatoes – squeeze on the juice of ½ lemon and serve. You can also add crumbled feta cheese, dill or mint leaves, or chopped olives (green or black) with the spinach. SERVES 4–6

SERVES 2

2 baking potatoes

sea salt flakes and freshly
ground black pepper

60g (2¼oz) cooked beetroot
(not pickled)

1 shallot, very finely
chopped

½ tablespoon chopped dill,
any coarse stalks removed

20g (¾oz) unsalted butter

75g (2¾oz) smoked trout,
flaked

good squeeze of lemon juice

60g (2¼oz) crème fraîche

25g (scant 1oz) keta
(salmon caviar)

bitter leaves, such as treviso
or red chicory, to serve

BAKED POTATOES WITH SMOKED TROUT, DILLED BEETROOT, CRÈME FRAÎCHE & KETA

It's mad, I know, but this dish – and it's just a fancy baked potato, really – is one of my favourites in the book. You don't have to have the salmon caviar, and it isn't cheap, but I love the little pearls of saltiness that pop in your mouth against the cream and the soft potato flesh.

Preheat the oven to 190°C fan (400°F), Gas Mark 6.

Scrub the potatoes and prick each with a fork. While they are still damp, sprinkle lightly all over with sea salt flakes. This will give a crisp skin (cooking them wrapped in foil will give a soft skin).

Put the potatoes on a baking sheet – not touching – and scatter the sheet with a little water by shaking wet hands over it. Bake for 1–1½ hours; the exact cooking time depends on the size of the potatoes and how many you are cooking at a time (more potatoes will take more time).

To test whether the potatoes are done, press them: they should feel soft under the skin and 'give' a little. Pierce with a fine skewer through to the centre, if you want to be sure.

While the potatoes are cooking, roughly chop the beetroot and toss with the shallot, dill and a little seasoning.

When the potatoes are ready, split them open, season and put some butter on both halves.

Fill with the beetroot mixture and the trout, squeeze lemon juice on top, then add a dollop of crème fraîche and spoon on some salmon caviar. Grind some pepper over the top and serve with a few bitter leaves.

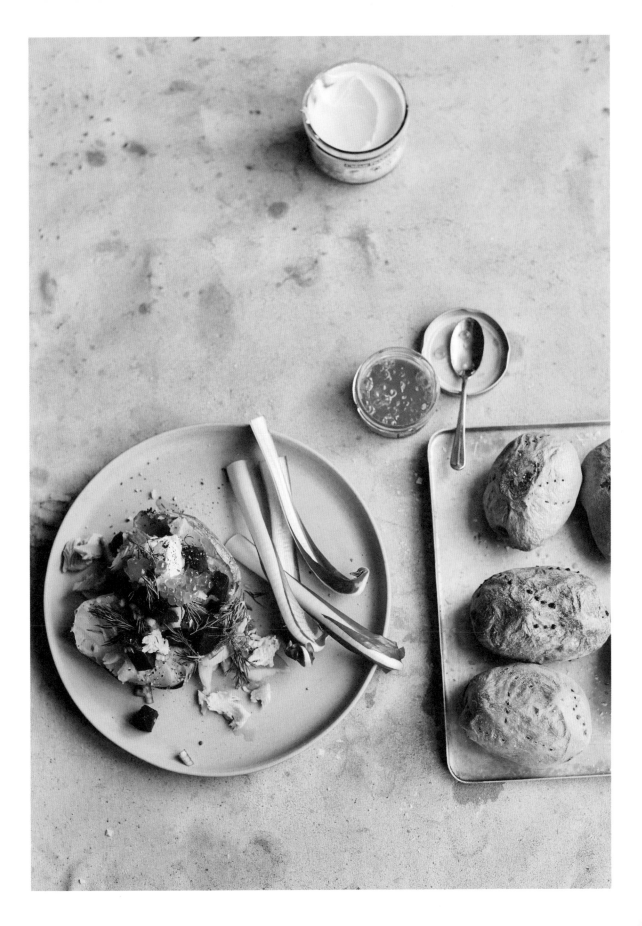

ROAST CAULIFLOWER WITH PISTACHIO & PRESERVED LEMON RELISH & TAHINI

SERVES 4, OR 8 AS A SIDE DISH

FOR THE CAULIFLOWER

1 large cauliflower, weighing about 1.2kg (2lb 12oz)

50g (1¾oz) unsalted butter, melted

7 tablespoons extra virgin olive oil

sea salt flakes and freshly ground black pepper

70ml (2½fl oz) tahini

juice of 1 lemon

1 garlic clove, finely grated

FOR THE RELISH

2 garlic cloves, chopped

pinch of sea salt flakes

35g (1¼oz) shelled unsalted pistachio nuts

30g (1oz) coriander leaves, chopped

8 tablespoons extra virgin olive oil

1 tablespoon cider vinegar

1 teaspoon runny honey

2 preserved lemons, rind only, finely shredded

2 green chillies, halved, deseeded and finely shredded

It took me a while to work out the best way to roast a whole cauliflower. Partly steaming it – which is what happens under the foil here – and then roasting it in butter (which seeps right down into the florets) produces the most tender and deeply flavoured result. I've been replacing olive oil with butter quite a lot – it cooks more gently, more richly, the surface of whatever it touches bathing in fat rather than frying in it. The cauliflower becomes tender right through to the middle and turns into a gorgeous golden mass.

Preheat the oven to 210°C fan (425°F), Gas Mark 7.

Carefully trim the cauliflower stalk, as it can be dry, but don't cut away the base or the leaves. Put it in a roasting tin in which it fits fairly snugly. Add boiling water to come 1cm (½in) up the sides and cover tightly with foil. Bake for 30 minutes (check to make sure the water hasn't dried up in this time). The cauliflower should just meet a little resistance when you push a skewer into the centre. Pour away any remaining water. Drizzle with the melted butter and 3 tablespoons of the olive oil and season. Roast, uncovered, for 15 minutes, or until the cauliflower is golden and the centre is completely tender (test with a skewer).

Beat the tahini in a bowl, adding 150ml (5fl oz) water, the lemon juice, the remaining 4 tablespoons of oil, salt and pepper and the garlic. The mixture will 'seize' when you add the lemon juice, but keep beating and you'll break it down into a smooth cream. Check for seasoning and acidity.

For the relish, put the garlic and salt in a mortar and pound until the garlic is completely crushed. Add the pistachios and coriander and bash everything together, gradually adding the oil and cider vinegar until you have a chunky paste (not a purée). Stir in the honey, preserved lemon rind and chillies.

Serve the cauliflower on a warmed platter and drizzle the tahini around it. Spoon the cooking juices and some relish on top, offering the rest on the side.

ROAST CABBAGE WEDGES WITH XO CRUMBS

SERVES 6 AS A STARTER,
OR AS A SIDE DISH

1 large round cabbage, such
as January King or Savoy, or
2 sweetheart cabbages

5 tablespoons extra virgin
olive oil, or 50g (1¾oz) pork
fat (available from Brindisa
in jars, or ask your butcher,
don't use lard)

65g (2½oz) rye sourdough
bread

3½ tablespoons XO sauce

Yes, XO sauce – a sauce made from dried scallops, shrimps and chilli that's popular in Hong Kong – is a specialist ingredient you'll probably have to buy online, but this dish is unique and I'd love you to taste it, without having to make the trip to St Leonard's restaurant in East London where they serve it. The chef there, Andrew Clarke, cooks cabbage wedges with pork fat on an open fire and makes his own XO sauce, but he helped me to work out this simpler version. The rye crumbs, tossed with the XO, are deeply umami (you must use rye crumbs). Who knew cabbage could be this good? I could eat it by the (large) plateful. If XO sauce is an adventure too far (or too spendy) you can still make roast cabbage wedges with a buttermilk dressing (see page 178), scattered with dill or smoked bacon lardons, or rye crumbs and caraway, or grated hard cheese (goat's milk gouda is gorgeous). You can also serve the wedges very simply, with grated Parmesan cheese.

Preheat the oven to 190°C fan (400°F), Gas Mark 6. Remove any discoloured leaves from the cabbage, then halve it and cut into wedges about 2.5–3cm (1–1¼in) thick. Melt the pork fat, if using, in a small saucepan. Put the cabbage into a roasting tin or oven tray. Add half the olive oil or fat and turn the wedges over in it. Roast for 30 minutes, turning halfway through.

Whizz the rye bread into coarse crumbs. Heat the remaining oil or fat in a large frying pan and, when hot, add the crumbs and sauté these until they're toasted (this is hard to tell by colour with rye crumbs, so try to go by texture and smell). Scrape these out on to a large double layer of kitchen paper to soak up the excess fat. Leave to cool, then transfer to a bowl and toss with the XO sauce, forking it through. (XO sauce isn't just liquid, it also has bits of dried shellfish in it, but you can still mix it in well.)

When the cabbage is tender and slightly caramelized – even a little scorched in patches – on each side, serve it with the XO crumbs scattered on top.

ROAST CAULIFLOWER WITH PARMA HAM & TALEGGIO CHEESE

SERVES 2–4, DEPENDING ON APPETITE

1 large cauliflower

a little extra virgin olive oil

sea salt flakes and freshly ground black pepper

125g (4½oz) Taleggio cheese, sliced

4 prosciutto slices

4 generous tablespoons crème fraîche

75g (2¾oz) Gruyère cheese, finely grated

salad leaves, to serve

Yes, a cauliflower 'steak' (though I refuse to call it that). I wasn't at all sure about roasting slices of cauliflower. It was another of those dishes that seemed to have been created just so we could think of vegetables as if they were meat, rather than being delicious in their own right... but then I made this for my children – the harshest critics – and they loved it. It's a bit of a cross between cauliflower cheese and veal Cordon Bleu and what's not to like about that? It will never be a steak because it isn't, but I like this just as much.

Preheat the oven to 220°C fan (450°F), Gas Mark 8.

Remove the leaves from the cauliflower. Now remove some of the central core, too – working at the base – so that you've lost the dense core (without cutting away so much that the head collapses). Cut the cauliflower in half from top to bottom, then cut off 4 slices – 2 from each half – each about 2cm (¾in) thick. Put these on a baking sheet, brush all over with olive oil and season. Cover the baking sheet with foil and cook for 12 minutes.

Remove the foil and reduce the oven temperature to 200°C fan (410°F), Gas Mark 6½. Roast the cauliflower for another 8 minutes.

Remove from the oven – the pieces should be golden – and turn the slices of cauliflower over. On top of each, lay one-quarter of the Taleggio, then a prosciutto slice, then 1 tablespoon crème fraîche. Sprinkle the slices evenly with the Gruyère and return to the oven.

Roast for another 8 minutes, or until the cauliflower is golden and all the cheese has melted. The cauliflower slices should be completely tender when pierced with a sharp knife.

Serve immediately with lightly dressed salad leaves.

OLIVE OIL-ROAST SWEET & SOUR LEAVES WITH RAISINS & PINE NUTS

SERVES 6–8 AS A
SIDE DISH

1 head of radicchio

250g (9oz) spring onions,
trimmed

sea salt flakes and freshly
ground black pepper

½ teaspoon chilli flakes

4 tablespoons extra virgin
olive oil

1½ tablespoons white
balsamic vinegar

400g (14oz) cavolo nero

2 garlic cloves, very finely
sliced

2 tablespoons raisins,
soaked in boiling water for
15 minutes, then drained

15g (½oz) toasted pine nuts

The timings for the cavolo nero here are crucial; the first time you make it you need to keep an eye on the leaves, because your oven could be slightly hotter or slightly cooler than it says on the dial. They can go from slightly scorched to burned very quickly. If you want a straighter version – not sweet-sour – then just leave out the raisins. In that case, you could finish the leaves with shaved Parmesan or pecorino cheese.

Preheat the oven to 210°C fan (425°F), Gas Mark 7.

Halve the radicchio and cut it into wedges. Remove the coarse core from each piece, but don't take away so much that the wedges fall apart. If any of the spring onions are thick, halve them lengthways.

Put the radicchio and the spring onions into a roasting tin and add salt and pepper, half the chilli, half the olive oil and 1 tablespoon of the white balsamic vinegar. Turn everything over with your hands (don't worry if some of the radicchio leaves break off).

Remove the stems from the cavolo nero and put it into another roasting tin. Add another 1 tablespoon of olive oil and the rest of the white balsamic vinegar and chilli and season. Put the radicchio in the oven and roast it for 5 minutes, then turn the pieces over and return it to the oven with the tin of cavolo nero alongside. Roast for 3 minutes, but no longer: timing is crucial. The cavolo nero should be slightly crispy around the edges, but mostly soft.

During this last 3 minutes, heat the last 1 tablespoon of olive oil in a frying pan and sauté the garlic until it's golden, then add the drained raisins and warm them through. Toss all the vegetables in a warmed serving dish, scatter with the garlic, raisins and pine nuts and serve immediately.

BAKED SWEET POTATOES WITH AVOCADO & CHIMICHURRI

Sweet, hot and salty, all the things I love eating together. If you can get hold of queso fresco – *Mexican cheese – use that instead, but feta, Lancashire and Wensleydale cheeses are all good (if not perfect) substitutes. Chimichurri, traditionally served with steak in Argentina and Uruguay, is most commonly made with parsley, but I like it better with half parsley and half coriander.*

Preheat the oven to 180°C fan (375°F), Gas Mark 5. Put the sweet potatoes on a metal baking sheet (line it with foil or baking parchment to save on the washing up, as the sugar in sweet potatoes can leach out and caramelize). Bake for 40 minutes, or until tender right through to the centre.

Put everything for the chimichurri into a blender and blitz to make a smooth sauce. Taste for seasoning.

Split the sweet potatoes down the centre, spoon in the yogurt or soured cream and sprinkle with the cheese and spring onions.

Halve the avocados, remove the stones and the skins, then slice or chop the flesh or scoop it straight on to the potatoes. Squeeze lemon or lime juice on the avocado flesh and season. Spoon on the chimichurri and serve, with lime wedges.

FOR THE VEGETABLES

4 sweet potatoes, each about 330g (11½oz), well scrubbed

about 125g (4½oz) Greek yogurt, or soured cream

35g (1¼oz) cheese (*queso fresco*, feta, Lancashire or Wensleydale), coarsely grated or crumbled

4 spring onions, trimmed and chopped on the diagonal

2 smallish ripe avocados

juice of ½ lemon or 1 lime, plus lime wedges to serve

FOR THE CHIMICHURRI

10g (¼oz) flat leaf parsley leaves

10g (¼oz) coriander leaves

leaves from 2 oregano sprigs (omit these if you don't have any)

2 garlic cloves, chopped

juice of ½ lemon

1 teaspoon chilli flakes

100ml (3½fl oz) extra virgin olive oil

sea salt flakes and freshly ground black pepper

ROAST JERUSALEM ARTICHOKES & LEEKS WITH CRÈME FRAÎCHE, SHAVED GOUDA & HAZELNUTS

You need fat Jerusalem artichokes for this, as thinner specimens just aren't fleshy enough. If you can't get quality Gouda, or don't want to use it, other hard cheeses (such as Lincolnshire Poacher) work, too. This is a gorgeous combination of flavours; don't leave out the hazelnuts as they really are key. This is one of my favourite dishes in the book.

Preheat the oven to 190°C fan (400°F), Gas Mark 6.

Halve the fatter artichokes lengthways and put all of them into a roasting tin in which they can lie in a single layer. Season and toss with half the olive oil. Turn everything over with your hands and roast for about 30 minutes.

Toss the leeks in the rest of the oil and season them. Add them to the roasting tin and cook for a final 10 minutes. The leeks should be tender and the artichokes completely soft and slightly sticky in places (the sugar in them oozes out in little patches).

Mix together the crème fraîche and the buttermilk or milk. Mixing will make the crème fraîche much thinner. Set aside.

To make a dressing, just mix the wine vinegar, mustard, seasoning, sugar and both the oils together and beat with a fork. Taste, as you might want to adjust the sweetness or acidity.

Toss the treviso or chicory with the dressing. Put the roast vegetables on a serving platter or shallow dish, scatter the treviso or chicory over them, then spoon on the crème fraîche mixture (or offer it on the side). Toss the hazelnuts and shaved cheese on top and serve.

SERVES 4 AS A SIDE DISH, OR AS A STARTER

FOR THE VEGETABLES

700g (1lb 9oz) fat Jerusalem artichokes, all about the same size

sea salt flakes and freshly ground black pepper

3–4 tablespoons extra virgin olive oil

270g (9½oz) baby leeks

150g (5½oz) crème fraîche

2 tablespoons buttermilk, or regular whole milk

1 head of treviso, or red chicory, leaves separated

25g (scant 1oz) toasted hazelnuts, halved

25g (scant 1oz) really good-quality Gouda cheese, shaved

FOR THE DRESSING

3 teaspoons red wine vinegar, or to taste

smidgen of Dijon mustard, or to taste

pinch of caster sugar, or to taste

1½ tablespoons extra virgin olive oil (a buttery oil, not a grassy one)

1½ tablespoons hazelnut or walnut oil

ROAST INDIAN-SPICED VEGETABLES WITH LIME-CORIANDER BUTTER

The next time you fancy an Indian takeaway (usually, for me, on a Friday evening, when I'm exhausted), make this instead. You just need to slice some vegetables, then it's 25 minutes in the oven. It is the simplest, loveliest dish: beautiful (the colour of the vegetables, especially with the red-and-green-flecked butter melting over them), earthy and aromatic. Serve it with natural yogurt (Greek yogurt is too creamy, you want something acidic to cut the sweet vegetables), with nigella seeds sprinkled on top, and some chutney (fresh, see page 106, or bought). You don't really need more starch, but warm naan bread is good, too.

Preheat the oven to 210°C fan (425°F), Gas Mark 7. Get out a huge roasting tin or baking sheet with a lip round the edge (the tin I use measures 38 x 36cm / 15 x 14in), or use a couple of smaller tins. Put the tin or tins in the oven to heat up.

Put all the vegetables in a very large bowl and add the garlic, oil and seasoning. Toast the cumin and coriander seeds in a dry frying pan for about a minute, or until you can smell the spices. Put the spices into a mortar with the turmeric and pound all this together. Add the spices to the vegetables in the bowl and turn everything over in the oil. Take the hot tin or tins out of the oven and tumble the vegetables into them. Roast for 25 minutes, tossing the vegetables around halfway through.

Mash the butter together with the chilli, coriander, lime zest and juice.

When the vegetables are ready, either transfer them to a warmed broad shallow bowl, or serve them in the tin in which they were cooked. Put knobs of the butter all over the top and allow it to melt.

Take the vegetables to the table and serve with natural yogurt and chutney.

SERVES 4

FOR THE VEGETABLES

300g (10½oz) small waxy potatoes, scrubbed and quartered

3 medium-small ready-cooked beetroot, halved

6 long slim carrots, halved (or 3 large carrots, quartered, if you can't find slim)

1 medium-large cauliflower, about 1kg (2lb 4oz), broken into florets, with the leaves

3 parsnips, halved lengthways

3 garlic cloves, finely grated

5 tablespoons groundnut oil

sea salt flakes and freshly ground black pepper

2 teaspoons cumin seeds

2 teaspoons coriander seeds

¾ teaspoon ground turmeric

natural yogurt and chutney, to serve

FOR THE BUTTER

75g (2¾oz) unsalted butter, at room temperature

1 red chilli, halved, deseeded and finely chopped, or ½ teaspoon chilli flakes

2 tablespoons finely chopped coriander leaves

finely grated zest of 1 lime, plus a squeeze of lime juice

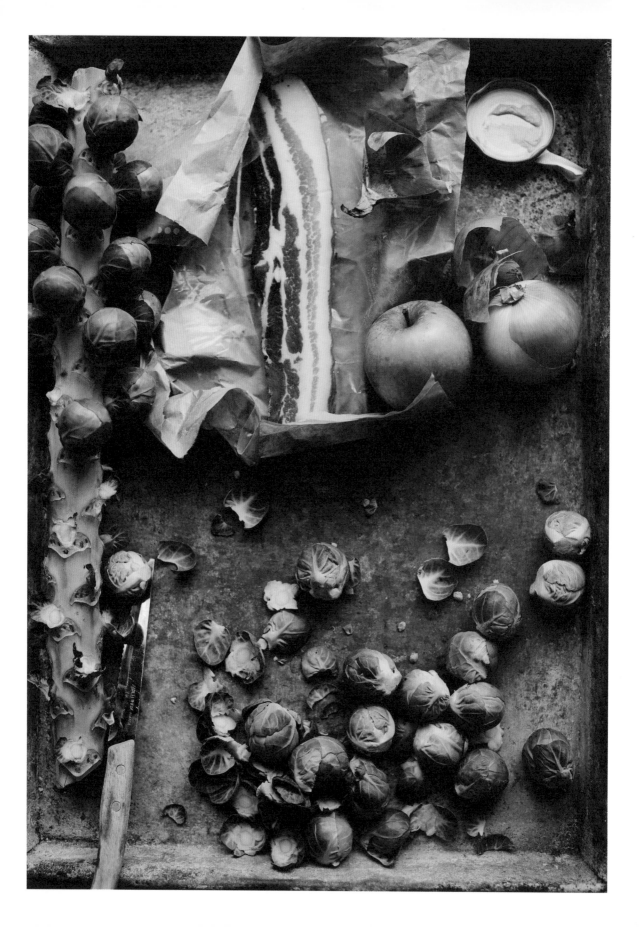

ROAST BRUSSELS SPROUTS WITH APPLE & BACON

SERVES 6 AS A SIDE DISH

700g (1lb 9oz) Brussels sprouts, any discoloured outer leaves removed, trimmed and halved

2¼ tablespoons extra virgin olive oil

sea salt flakes and freshly ground black pepper

200g (7oz) bacon lardons

1 large tart eating apple, such as Granny Smith

1 large onion, cut into fine crescent moons

½ tablespoon soft light brown sugar

1 tablespoon white balsamic vinegar

1 tablespoon cider vinegar

125ml (4fl oz) dry white wine

3 teaspoons Dijon mustard

10g (¼oz) unsalted butter (optional, you may feel this is gilding the lily)

I'm cheating here, because this isn't entirely cooked in the oven, but the brief roasting is what helps Brussels sprouts achieve their optimum potential, instead of waterlogging them in a saucepan. I ate a similar dish at Rotisserie Georgette in New York – a restaurant that specializes in roast chicken – then came straight home and made this. It's been a regular in my house ever since, and not just at Christmas.

Preheat the oven to 180°C fan (375°F), Gas Mark 5.

Lay the sprouts in a single layer in 1 or 2 roasting tins. Add 2 tablespoons of olive oil, season and toss.

Roast for 20 minutes, or until the edges begin to look brown and frazzled (they can turn from frazzled to burned very quickly, so keep an eye on them). They won't cook right through, but will finish cooking later.

Heat the remaining ¼ tablespoon more oil in a sauté pan and fry the bacon lardons until golden and cooked through. Lift out with a slotted spoon.

Remove all but 1 tablespoon of fat from the pan (fat will have rendered from the bacon). Core the apple and cut it into fine crescents, then add to the pan with the onion. Cook over a medium heat until golden and soft (though the apple shouldn't be collapsing). It will take about 5 minutes.

Add the sugar, both vinegars, the wine and mustard. Return the bacon and season to taste. Toss well and cook until the wine has reduced by about half, then add the sprouts and cook until they are only just tender, but not floppy (all the juices around them should have reduced).

Toss in the butter, if you're using it. Check the seasoning and serve.

ROAST MUSHROOMS, JERUSALEM ARTICHOKES & CELERIAC WITH BROWN BUTTER & HORSERADISH

SERVES 4 AS PART OF A SPREAD OF DISHES

600g (1lb 5oz) Jerusalem artichokes, all about the same size

500g (1lb 2oz) celeriac, peeled and cut into 1cm (½in) wedges

3 tablespoons extra virgin olive oil

100g (3½oz) unsalted butter, melted, plus 25g (scant 1oz) to serve

sea salt flakes and freshly ground black pepper

8 big flat field mushrooms, trimmed

15g (½oz) fresh horseradish, peeled and finely grated, or to taste

crème fraîche, to serve

Roast mushrooms, celeriac and Jerusalem artichokes look lovely together – a tumble of autumnal beige and brown – and there's a lovely interplay of sweetness, savoury meatiness and herby flavours. I always find Jerusalem artichokes too sweet, and celeriac too herbal, when I have them on their own. This is a great recipe for very cold weather, when it doesn't seem overly rich, despite the butter and crème fraîche.

Preheat the oven to 190°C fan (400°F), Gas Mark 6.

Scrub the Jerusalem artichokes. You don't need to peel them, but halve any larger ones lengthways. Put them and the celeriac into a roasting tin in which they can lie in a single layer. Mix the oil and the 100g (3½oz) melted butter and pour about half over the vegetables. Season and toss, then roast for about 45 minutes in total, turning the vegetables over so that they become golden on both sides.

Put the mushrooms into a roasting tin where they can lie in a single layer and pour on the rest of the fat. Turn these over with your hands, too, and roast alongside the celeriac and Jerusalem artichokes until they are dark and shrunken, about 30 minutes. The celeriac and Jerusalem artichokes should be tender when pierced with a sharp knife.

Transfer the vegetables to a warmed platter or bowl; you can either leave the mushrooms whole or tear them roughly.

To serve, heat the 25g (scant 1oz) butter until it is golden brown and smells nutty. Pour this over the vegetables and scatter with the horseradish, adding more if you like its clean heat. Serve with a bowl of crème fraîche.

POMEGRANATE MOLASSES-ROAST BEETROOT WITH ORANGES, WALNUTS, DILL & LABNEH

SERVES 8 AS A SIDE DISH

If you don't want to make the labneh here – and you need to make it the day before – then just serve thick yogurt instead. Blood oranges are especially good, so use them if they're in season. I've suggested buying beetroot with the leaves attached, but that isn't always possible, so just cook what you can find.

Put the yogurt into a piece of muslin or a brand new all-purpose kitchen cloth set in a sieve over a bowl. Stir in some salt and pepper. Pull the fabric up round the yogurt to make a 'bag'. Put the whole thing – including the bowl to catch the moisture that drains out – in the fridge for 24 hours. Give it a gentle squeeze every so often. You'll get a firm yogurt 'cheese'.

Preheat the oven to 190°C fan (400°F), Gas Mark 6. Wash and peel the beetroot, keeping the leaves intact, and halve any that are a bit larger. Put a double layer of foil (big enough to make a tent around the beetroot) into a roasting tin. Mix the balsamic vinegar, olive oil, pomegranate molasses and garlic together and season well. Put the beets into the foil and pour this on. Toss, then seal the foil to make a package. Cook in the oven until tender right to the middle. This can take as much as 90 minutes, but start checking after 40 (cooking time for beetroot varies hugely, but you can make these in advance, as they're served at room temperature).

Whisk together all the ingredients for the dressing, then taste for seasoning. Cut the beetroot into wedges, keeping any leaves intact, and toss them in a bowl with half the dressing, then transfer to a serving platter. Add the orange segments or slices.

Spoon the rest of the dressing over – only use as much as you need, don't smother the beetroots – then scatter with the pomegranate seeds, walnuts and dill. Break the labneh into chunks and dot it around. (If you're using thick yogurt instead, dot spoonfuls here and there, or serve it on the side.)

FOR THE LABNEH AND VEGETABLES

150g (5½oz) Greek yogurt

sea salt flakes and freshly ground black pepper

1.5kg (3lb 5oz) medium-small beetroot with leaves

2 tablespoons white balsamic vinegar

3 tablespoons extra virgin olive oil

2 tablespoons pomegranate molasses

1 garlic clove, finely grated

3 small oranges, skin, pith and seeds removed, cut into neat segments or slices

seeds from ½ pomegranate

2 tablespoons roughly chopped toasted walnuts

leaves from a small bunch of dill, roughly chopped

FOR THE DRESSING

1 tablespoon white balsamic vinegar

1 teaspoon harissa (or more, depending how hot you want it)

5 tablespoons extra virgin olive oil

½ teaspoon runny honey

½ tablespoon pomegranate molasses

ROAST SQUASH & TOFU WITH SOY, HONEY, CHILLI & GINGER

I love the flavours here: sweet and hot. This can be served as a side dish, or as a main course with rice on the side. It doesn't strictly need a sauce, but a hot Asian dressing (see page 194) would be excellent, if you want that.

Preheat the oven to 200°C fan (410°F), Gas Mark 6½.

Drain the tofu and cut it into 1.5cm (⅝in) thick slices. Put a double layer of kitchen paper on a chopping board, add the tofu, then put another double layer of kitchen paper on top. Place another chopping board on top of this and weight it. Leave for 20 minutes, to press out excess moisture.

Halve and deseed the squash and cut it into wedges about 1.5–2cm (⅝–¾in) thick. In a small bowl, mix the honey, soy sauce, chilli flakes, ginger and 75ml (2½fl oz) of the oil together.

Divide the squash between 2 roasting tins or trays – you can line them with baking parchment if you want, as it makes the dishes easier to clean – and spoon two-thirds of the soy sauce mixture over it. Turn the squash slices over with your hands.

Cut the tofu slices in half and put them in a smaller roasting tin. Spoon the rest of the soy sauce mixture over this, turning the pieces in it. Season the squash and tofu and roast in the oven for 15 minutes.

Turn the squash and tofu chunks over. Mix the remaining oil with the garlic and spoon over the squash, then roast with the tofu for a final 10–15 minutes, until the tofu is dark and the squash is burnished and completely tender.

Arrange the squash and tofu on a warmed serving plate, scatter with the sesame seeds and spring onions and squeeze over the lime juice. Serve.

SERVES 6 WITH RICE, OR AS A SIDE DISH

450g (1lb) extra-firm tofu

900g (2lb) squash, ideally Crown Prince, if you can get it

3 tablespoons runny honey

6 tablespoons soy sauce

2 teaspoons chilli flakes

2cm (¾in) fresh root ginger, peeled and finely grated

125ml (4fl oz) groundnut oil

sea salt flakes and freshly ground black pepper

6 garlic cloves, very finely sliced

3 teaspoons toasted sesame seeds

2 spring onions, trimmed and sliced on the diagonal

juice of ½ lime

ROAST CELERIAC & SPROUTS WITH BACON, CHESTNUTS & PRUNES

It doesn't have to be eaten just during the festive season, but this dish does shout 'CHRISTMAS' rather loudly. You need really good-quality moist prunes, so, as you're not shelling out for fillet of beef or the like here, buy Agen prunes if you can.

Preheat the oven to 190°C fan (400°F), Gas Mark 6.

Peel the celeriac and cut it into chunks no bigger than the size of the halved sprouts (larger chunks won't cook through in time). Toss it in a large roasting tin with salt and pepper, half the oil and all the vinegar and thyme.

Roast for 20 minutes, then stir the celeriac around and add the sprouts, onion, pancetta and the rest of the oil.

Roast for another 10 minutes, then add the chestnuts, prunes, sherry, maple syrup and butter and toss the vegetables around.

Cook for a final 10 minutes, then serve.

600g (1lb 5oz) celeriac

sea salt flakes and freshly ground black pepper

3 tablespoons extra virgin olive oil

1 tablespoon sherry vinegar

6 thyme sprigs

600g (1lb 5oz) good-sized Brussels sprouts, any discoloured outer leaves removed, trimmed and halved

1 large onion, cut into slim wedges

125g (4½oz) pancetta or bacon, cut into chunky lardons

125g (4½oz) cooked chestnuts

100g (3½oz) prunes, halved

75ml (2½fl oz) amontillado sherry

1 tablespoon maple syrup

10g (¼oz) unsalted butter

ROAST PURPLE SPROUTING BROCCOLI WITH CREAM & PARMESAN CHEESE

SERVES 4 AS A SIDE DISH,
OR AS PART OF A SPREAD
OF DISHES

400g (14oz) purple sprouting broccoli

1½ tablespoons extra virgin olive oil

sea salt flakes and freshly ground black pepper

25g (scant 1oz) unsalted butter

60g (2¼oz) fresh white breadcrumbs

300ml (½ pint) double cream

30g (1oz) Parmesan cheese, or half Parmesan and half Gruyère, finely grated

I love roast purple sprouting broccoli served in all sorts of ways – with feta cheese and chopped preserved lemon scattered over, or with chopped fried anchovies, garlic and chilli – but this has all the deliciousness of a gratin without using quite as much cream. You could also add chopped anchovies and a finely grated garlic clove, or a couple of sautéed shallots, to the cream and pour this over the broccoli (there's no need to add the Parmesan cheese if you do this).

Preheat the oven to 190°C fan (400°F), Gas Mark 6.

Trim the bases of the broccoli stalks. If any of the spears are thick, halve them along their length.

Put these into a roasting tin or on to a baking sheet with a lip and toss with the olive oil and seasoning. Roast for 12 minutes.

Melt the butter in a frying pan. Add the breadcrumbs and turn them over until they are buttery, but not toasted.

Pour the cream over the broccoli, season and sprinkle on the cheese and the buttered crumbs. Return to the oven and roast for a final 10–11 minutes, or until golden and bubbling. Serve straight away.

SALAD OF ROAST CARROTS, APPLE & LENTILS WITH CHILLI & PRESERVED LEMONS

I know this sounds odd, but it works, and it works as a main course lunch salad, not just as a supporting side dish. The real surprise of this recipe is just how good apples are with chillies and preserved lemons.

Preheat the oven to 200°C fan (410°F), Gas Mark 6½.

Trim the carrots, but leave a bit of green tuft. If you can't find young carrots, halve or quarter larger ones lengthways. Don't peel them, just wash them well. Place in a single layer in a roasting tin. Add the olive oil, salt and pepper, then toss to ensure the carrots are coated.

Roast in the oven for 30–35 minutes, or until tender. Be careful not to overcook them.

Make the dressing by putting the vinegar in a bowl and whisking in all the other ingredients with a fork. Season.

Put the lentils into a broad shallow serving bowl with half the chilli and one-third of the preserved lemon. Season a little, then toss with about one-third of the dressing.

Halve and core the apple or apples (there's no need to peel them) and cut into matchsticks. Throw into a large mixing bowl with the lemon juice and add the carrots. Add the rest of the preserved lemons and chilli, along with two-thirds of the herbs and the remaining dressing.

Throw the rest of the mint and coriander into the lentils. Put the carrot and apple mixture on top – you should still be able to see the lentils around the sides – and serve.

FOR THE SALAD

350g (12oz) young carrots (a mixture of colours is best, if you can find them)

3 tablespoons extra virgin olive oil

sea salt flakes and freshly ground black pepper

245g (8¾oz) cooked Puy lentils (you can buy them in pouches)

1 red and 1 green chilli, halved, deseeded and very finely shredded

2 preserved lemons, rind only, finely shredded, plus 2 teaspoons brine from the jar

1 large or 2 medium tart eating apples

juice of ½ lemon

leaves from 10 mint sprigs, torn

leaves from 15g (½oz) bunch of coriander

FOR THE DRESSING

2 tablespoons white balsamic vinegar

6 tablespoons extra virgin olive oil (fruity rather than grassy)

1 fat garlic clove, finely grated

1cm (½in) fresh root ginger, peeled and finely grated

¼ teaspoon runny honey

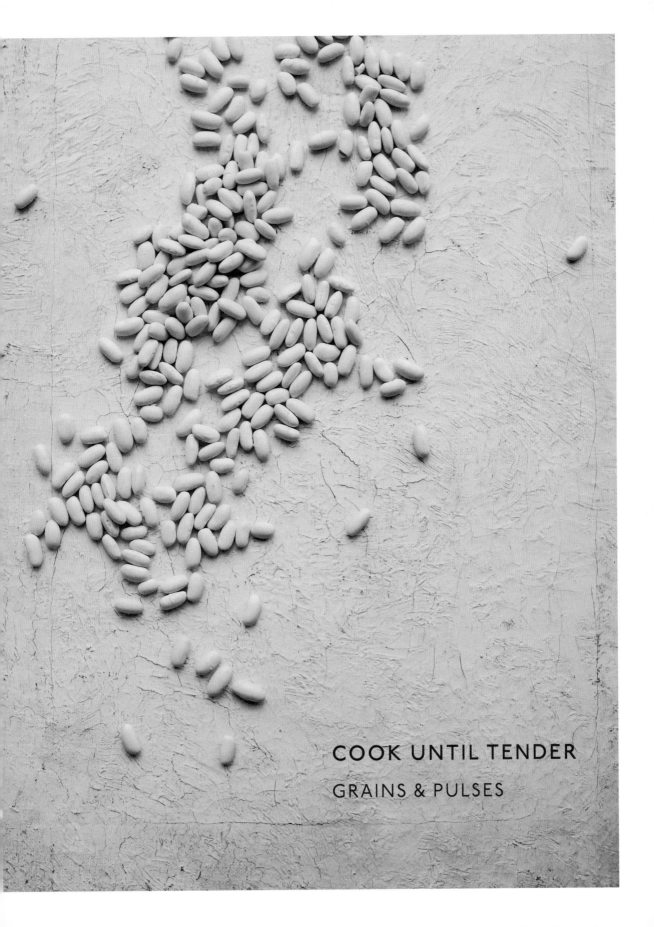

COOK UNTIL TENDER

GRAINS & PULSES

SAUSAGES & LENTILS WITH HERB RELISH

Why bake the lentils for this, rather than cook them on the stove top? Well, because they become imbued with the juices from the sausages and they keep their shape better, each lentil a perfect little lens. They also seem to taste much more intense than any pulses I cook on the hob. You have to use exactly the size of dish stipulated, so that the lentils – and the stock in which they're baking – cook at the right rate.

Preheat the oven to 180°C fan (375°F), Gas Mark 5.

Heat the olive oil in a 30cm (12in) ovenproof sauté pan and brown the sausages all over (you just need to colour them, not cook them through). Lift the sausages out. Add the onion, celery, carrot and pancetta or bacon lardons to the pan and sauté until the bacon is golden. Separately mix the stock and wine or cider together in a jug.

Add the garlic and lentils to the pan with the bay leaves and toss with the vegetables, then add 550ml (1 pint) of the stock mixture. Bring to the boil, season, return the sausages, then transfer to the oven.

Cook, uncovered, for 15 minutes. Stir and add the rest of the stock mixture, then cover and bake for a final 25–30 minutes. The lentils should be tender and the liquid almost completely absorbed. Taste for seasoning, though the reduced stock, wine and bacon should have made the dish quite salty enough.

Make the relish. Either chop the herbs and capers finely and mix with the other ingredients, or whizz everything together in a food processor. Taste for seasoning.

Serve the sausages and lentils with the relish. Offer Dijon mustard and crusty bread on the side.

SERVES 4

FOR THE SAUSAGES AND LENTILS

1½ tablespoons extra virgin olive oil

8 good-quality pork sausages

1 onion, finely chopped

½ celery stick, finely chopped

1 medium carrot, finely chopped

125g (4½oz) pancetta or bacon lardons

500ml (18fl oz) chicken stock

350ml (12fl oz) dry white wine or cider

1 garlic clove, finely grated

275g (9¾oz) Puy lentils

2 bay leaves

sea salt flakes and freshly ground black pepper

Dijon mustard and crusty bread, to serve

FOR THE RELISH

50g (1¾oz) soft herb leaves such as flat leaf parsley, basil, mint, chives, or a mix of whatever you have

1½ tablespoons capers, rinsed, drained and patted dry

2 garlic cloves, very finely chopped

½ teaspoon Dijon mustard

juice of 1 lemon

7 tablespoons extra virgin olive oil

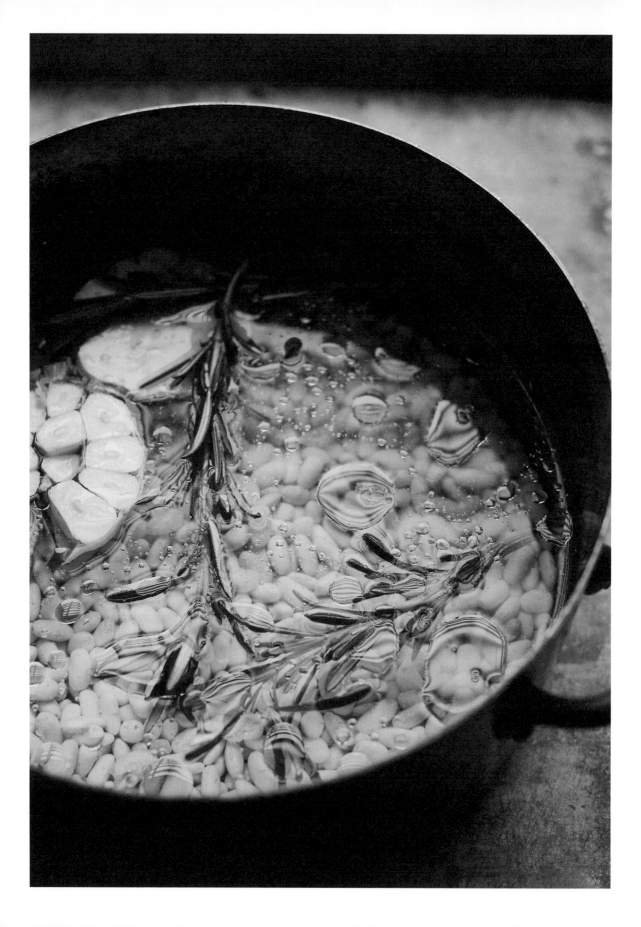

OVEN-BAKED BEANS WITH ROSEMARY & CHILLI

SERVES 8

500g (1lb 2oz) dried cannellini or haricot beans

1 celery stick, finely chopped

4 large rosemary sprigs

2 large carrots, halved lengthways

1 large onion, quartered

2 heads of garlic, halved horizontally

4 tablespoons extra virgin olive oil

sea salt flakes and freshly ground black pepper

3½ tablespoons tomato purée

1 teaspoon chilli flakes

handful of white breadcrumbs (optional)

You do have to start these beans off on the hob – getting them to simmering point – before transferring them to the oven, but I much prefer them being baked behind that closed door. They keep their shape better and their flavour really intensifies. You might need to add liquid, depending on how soupy or how thick you want the end result to be. You can also thicken the beans simply by continuing to cook them without a lid, or by adding breadcrumbs.

Put the beans in a large bowl, cover with plenty of cold water and leave to soak overnight.

The next day, preheat the oven to 140°C fan (300°F), Gas Mark 2.

Drain the beans and put them into a large ovenproof saucepan with the celery, rosemary, carrots, onion, garlic and olive oil. Add plenty of pepper and enough water to cover the beans by about 4cm (1½in). Bring to the boil on the hob, then transfer, uncovered, to the oven. Bake for 1 hour, checking every so often to see that the beans are moist.

Now you can remove the carrots if you want to. I usually leave one in and chop it roughly with a knife (just in the pot) and remove the other. The chopped one eventually disintegrates and helps the sauce around the beans to thicken, but not everyone likes the sweetness of the carrot and you might prefer the dish to taste more purely of beans.

Add the tomato purée, chilli and some salt to the saucepan and stir. Return the pot to the oven, again uncovered, and cook for a final hour. The top will become glossy and thick and almost slightly dry. When that happens, stir the beans: that skin forming on the top is delicious and you want to distribute it. You can cook the beans until they are as thick as you want them, or you can add breadcrumbs for the last 10 minutes or so to thicken them (if you do add breadcrumbs, adjust the seasoning again, as the dish may need more salt).

BAKED BABY PUMPKINS STUFFED WITH WILD MUSHROOMS, LEEKS, GRAINS & LINCOLNSHIRE POACHER CHEESE

This is the kind of dish that can be a bit of a hassle by the time you've sautéed and roasted the various components, so I've tried to simplify it. You can cook the grains yourself, of course (lentils are also good), but I often use ready-cooked packs. When small pumpkins aren't in season, bigger ones are fine, they just take more time to become tender before you add the stuffing.

Preheat the oven to 190°C fan (400°F), Gas Mark 6. Cut the tops off the pumpkins so that each has a 'lid', then remove the seeds and fibres from inside with a spoon. Rub the butter inside and season the insides, too, with salt, pepper and nutmeg. Put in a roasting tin – along with the 'lids' – and bake for 15 minutes, or until the flesh is soft when pierced with a knife.

Put the dried mushrooms into a bowl and add just enough boiling water to cover. Leave these to plump up for 20 minutes. Arrange the chestnut mushrooms in a roasting tin or on a baking sheet (one with a lip) in a single layer. It will look like a lot, but they shrink. Toss with 3 tablespoons of olive oil, season and roast for 30 minutes. Mushrooms throw out a lot of water, but it will evaporate, and they should become quite dark. Put the leeks in another roasting tin in 1 layer, toss with the remaining 1½ tablespoons of oil, season and roast alongside the mushrooms for 10–15 minutes. They should be tender. Chop them into 3cm (1¼in) lengths.

Stir the grains, leeks, roast mushrooms and dried mushrooms together, adding the mushroom soaking liquid. Add the thyme, garlic and two-thirds of the cheese. Taste for seasoning. You can prepare the recipe up to this stage in advance, then assemble and finish cooking it at the last minute.

Fill the pumpkins with the stuffing. Drizzle the cream into each and scatter on the remaining cheese. Bake for 10 minutes, or until they are soft and the cheesy tops are golden. Serve with the 'lids' on.

SERVES 8

8 little pumpkins, 10–12cm (4–4½in) in diameter

100g (3½oz) unsalted butter, slightly softened

sea salt flakes and freshly ground black pepper

freshly grated nutmeg

30g (1oz) dried wild mushrooms

500g (1lb 2oz) chestnut mushrooms, trimmed and halved

4½ tablespoons extra virgin olive oil

8 baby leeks, trimmed

250g (9oz) cooked grains (farro, barley or freekeh)

leaves from 2 thyme sprigs

1 garlic clove, finely grated

125g (4½oz) Lincolnshire Poacher cheese (Cheddar, Gruyère and Fontina also work), grated

230ml (8fl oz) double cream

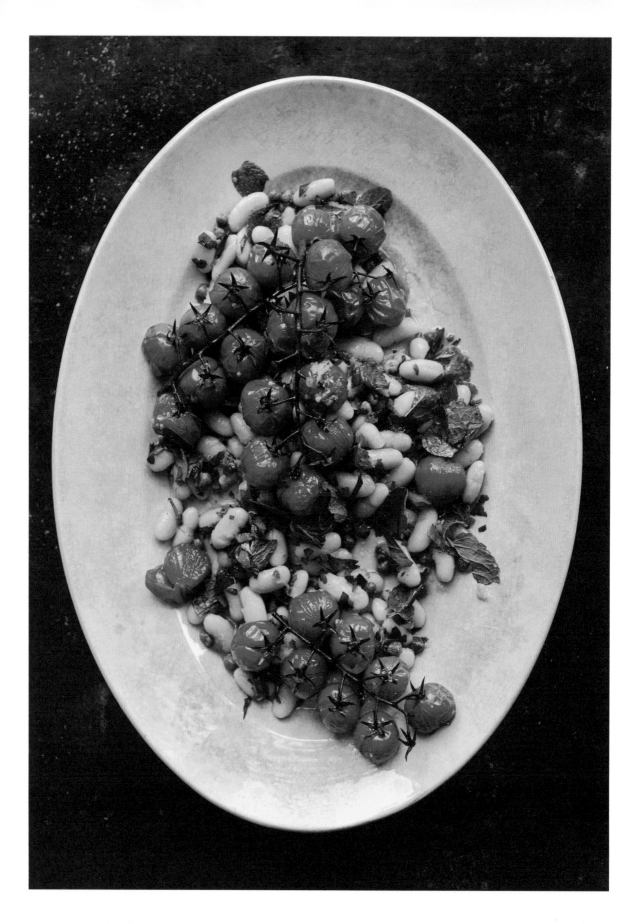

WHITE BEANS & ROAST TOMATOES WITH CAPER, MINT & CHILLI DRESSING

This is what I make when I have a load of cherry tomatoes that are slightly sagging – or a bit insipid – and need to be rescued. The oven condenses their sweetness.

Preheat the oven to 190°C fan (400°F), Gas Mark 6.

Make a dressing by mixing the mustard together with the white balsamic vinegar and some salt and pepper then, using a fork, whisk in 5 tablespoons of the olive oil. Add the chilli and garlic. Toss half of this in with the beans in a serving dish and leave to soak.

Put the cherry tomatoes in a roasting tin, drizzle with the remaining 2 tablespoons of oil, season and roast for 15 minutes. Leave them to cool a little.

If you're using mint or basil, just tear the leaves. If you're using parsley, chop it finely. Toss a little of this into the remaining dressing and add the rest of the herbs to the beans, along with the capers.

Lay the tomatoes on top of the beans, pouring on all their cooking juices, spoon over the remaining dressing and serve.

smidgen (about ¼ teaspoon or less) Dijon mustard

1¼ tablespoons white balsamic vinegar

sea salt flakes and freshly ground black pepper

7 tablespoons extra virgin olive oil

1 red chilli, halved, deseeded and finely chopped, or a good pinch of chilli flakes

1 small garlic clove, finely grated

400g can of cannellini beans, rinsed and left to drain and dry a little in a sieve

500g (1lb 2oz) cherry tomatoes on the vine

handful of mint, basil or flat leaf parsley leaves, or any soft herb leaves you have

1¼ tablespoons capers, rinsed, drained and patted dry

GRAINS ON THE SIDE...

Not every dish in this book has a starch incorporated into it, and I don't stretch my love of the oven to using it to cook foods that are better dealt with in another way (though there is a baked rice dish on page 156 which you can adapt at will). Here is a simple guide to cooking grains on the hob. Once drained, they can be mixed with melted butter or olive oil, herbs, nuts, crumbled cheese such as feta, or soaked and drained dried fruits.

WHITE LONG-GRAIN RICE Put the rice in a pan, cover it with 2.5cm (1in) water (for me that is about a third of my index finger, which is a good way to judge it) and bring to the boil. Boil hard until the water looks as if it has been absorbed and the surface of the rice is 'pitted' with little holes. Cover the pan, place it over the lowest heat and cook for 15–20 minutes (check after 15 minutes, lifting a few grains with a fork). It's important that you don't stir the rice until it's ready. Fork it through to aerate it before serving.

You can also cook rice in stock, which gives a much more intensely flavoured potful. Rinse the rice in a sieve until the water runs clear, then sauté a chopped onion in oil or butter until pale gold and soft. Stir in the rice, turning to coat in the fat, then pour in stock (350ml / 12fl oz for every 150g / 5½oz rice) and bring to the boil, uncovered. Now continue as above. You can flavour this with spices, garlic, hard herbs or citrus zest. If you're using spices and garlic, cook them for a few minutes once the onion is soft before adding the rice.

BROWN LONG-GRAIN RICE & CAMARGUE RED RICE Brown rice never softens the way white rice does, but retains a firm, nutty centre. Cook it in boiling water for about 25 minutes, then drain. Camargue red rice cooks in the same way, though it only takes 20–25 minutes, and has the same chewy texture and a similar flavour.

WILD RICE Wild rice is from a native American water grass. It's best mixed with another grain, because of its texture (on its own it is very chewy), and because it looks striking. Simmer it on its own – it turns the water purple-grey – for 35 minutes.

COUSCOUS Couscous isn't a grain, but a grain product, as it's made from rolled semolina. You can now buy a wholegrain version, as well as couscous made from barley or kamut. Just pour boiling water or stock over the grains – 175–200ml (6–7fl oz) of liquid to 200g (7oz) of couscous – cover with cling film and leave for 15 minutes. Finish with melted butter or olive oil and seasoning and fork it through to aerate it.

BULGUR WHEAT Quicker and easier than rice and gloriously nutty. It's made when wheat (usually durum) is boiled, dried, cracked, then sorted by size. Cook in boiling water or stock. The time it takes depends on the coarseness of the grain, so check after 10 minutes (medium cooks in 15 minutes), then fork it through to aerate it, cover and leave to stand for another 5 minutes. I generally cook it in stock, using twice the volume of liquid to grain.

FARRO & SPELT Farro is emmer wheat, a really old grain. The type most commonly available is semi-pearled (labelled *semi-perlato*). It doesn't need soaking and cooks in 20–25 minutes. The unpearled type, should you find it, needs to be soaked overnight and takes an hour to cook (it's quite like pot barley in both taste and appearance). Spelt is also an ancient wheat grain, and the two are often used interchangeably. Cook spelt just like semi-pearled farro.

FREEKEH This is roasted young green wheat, cooked mostly in the Middle East. It has a good assertive flavour – smoky and nutty – and a firm texture. Boil it in water for 20–25 minutes, then drain.

BARLEY Pearl barley is the type most commonly available. This has been processed: the germ and some of the bran has been removed. The unprocessed type, pot (or 'Scotch') barley, takes about an hour to cook (and needs to be soaked overnight beforehand). Pearl barley cooks in 25–30 minutes.

QUINOA This is often cooked with too much liquid, so you end up with something like gruel. Use 675ml (1 pint 4fl oz) water or stock for every 300g (10½oz) quinoa and cook gently – simmer, don't boil – for 15 minutes. It also helps the flavour if you toast the quinoa in a dry frying pan before you cook it.

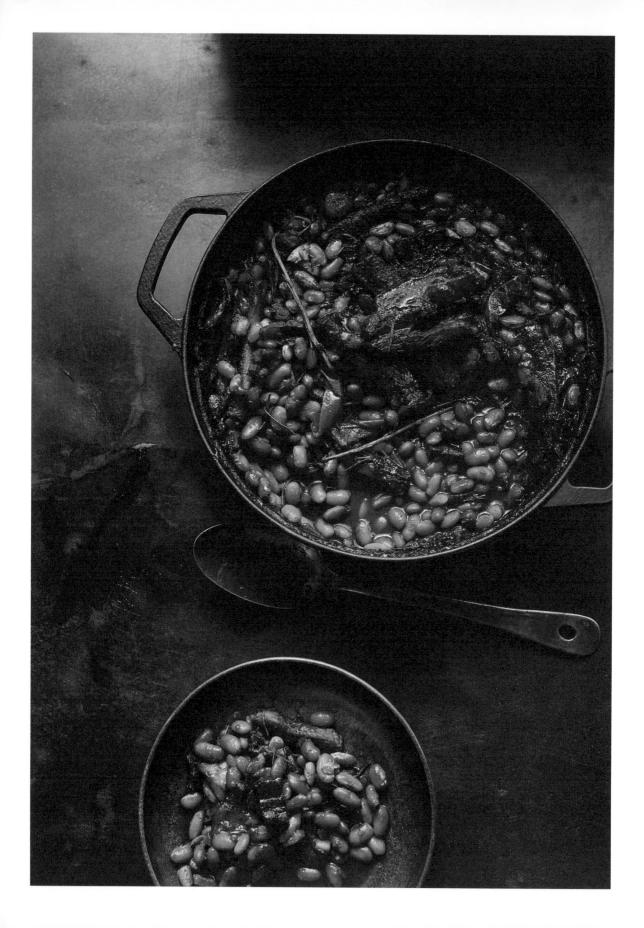

BAKED BEANS WITH SMOKED BACON, PORK BELLY & TREACLE

This is based on an American dish, Boston baked beans, but it contains a bit more meat than the original. I love the smokiness, but you can use unsmoked bacon if you prefer. This can be easily reheated... in fact, it tastes even better the next day.

Put the beans in a bowl, cover with plenty of water and soak overnight.

Preheat the oven to 140°C fan (300°F), Gas Mark 2.

Drain the beans. Tip them into a large ovenproof saucepan or casserole with the celery, half the rosemary, the carrots and quartered onion. Add plenty of pepper and enough water to cover by about 3cm (1¼in). Bring to the boil, cover and transfer to the oven. Bake for 1 hour.

Remove the carrots and celery. I usually just leave the onion, but fish it out if you want. Add the rest of the rosemary, the chopped onion and the garlic.

Heat the olive oil in a frying pan over a medium heat and brown the bacon and pork. Add these to the bean saucepan. Stir in the black treacle, mustard, sugar, tomato purée and chilli flakes and season well. Bring to the boil once more, then return to the oven, this time leaving it uncovered.

Bake for 3 hours – you might even need a bit longer – gently turning the beans over a couple of times during the cooking time and keeping an eye on the level of the liquid. You want the juices to reduce so that you are left with a thick mass, but you don't want the beans to get too dry. When they have 1 hour of cooking time left, add the cider vinegar, to cut the sweetness and add depth to the flavour. In the last hour of cooking, it's best to leave the beans alone, so they get a lovely baked crust on top.

Serve in warmed broad flat soup plates or pasta bowls. You don't need anything starchy with this – and the dish is usually served on its own – but I do like Savoy cabbage with it.

SERVES 8

500g (1lb 2oz) dried beans, such as cannellini, borlotti or pinto

1 celery stick

4 large rosemary sprigs

2 large carrots, halved lengthways

2 large onions, 1 quartered, 1 chopped

sea salt flakes and freshly ground black pepper

2 heads of garlic, halved horizontally

1 tablespoon extra virgin olive oil

200g (7oz) smoked bacon in 1 piece, cut into large chunks

400g (14oz) boneless pork belly slices, 2cm (¾in) thick, rind removed, halved

2 tablespoons black treacle

2 tablespoons Dijon mustard

3 tablespoons soft light brown sugar

2 tablespoons tomato purée

1–2 teaspoons chilli flakes, depending how spicy you want it

1–2 tablespoons cider vinegar, or to taste

Savoy cabbage, to serve (optional)

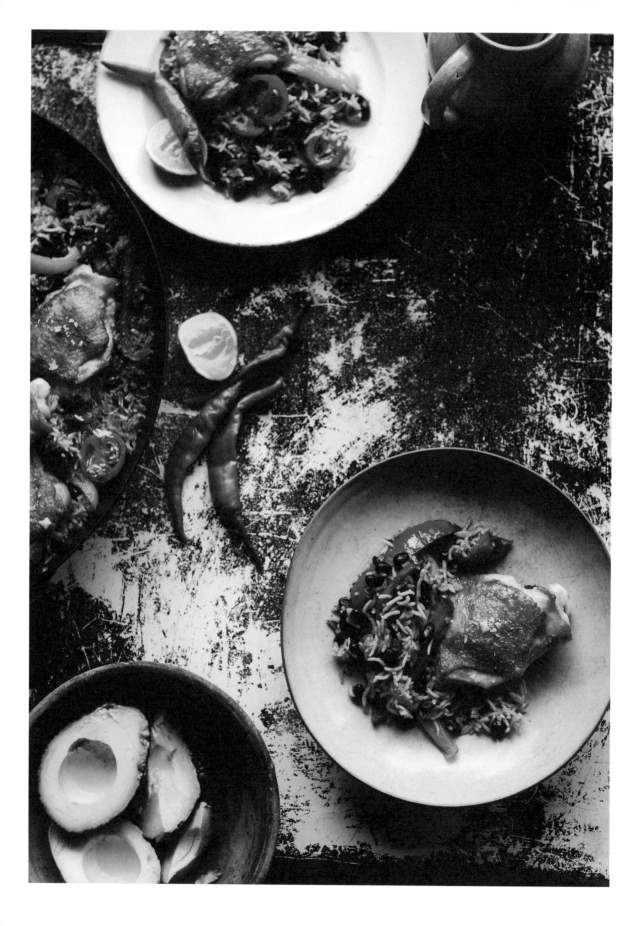

SOUTH AMERICAN-SPICED CHICKEN, BLACK BEANS & RICE WITH AVOCADO, PICKLED CHILLIES & SOURED CREAM

Another baked rice dish, so again you do need to cook it in the size of pan suggested. The chicken, beans and rice are, in themselves, simple, but it's the add-ons here that make the dish special, so don't overlook them.

Preheat the oven to 180°C fan (375°F), Gas Mark 5.

Heat the oil in a 30cm (12in) ovenproof sauté pan or shallow casserole (the size is very important) and quickly brown the chicken pieces on both sides, just to give them a good colour. Remove and set aside. Add the onion and peppers to the pan and sauté for 5 minutes, or until just starting to soften.

Add the garlic, cumin, cinnamon and chillies and cook for about 2 minutes, then add the black beans and cherry tomatoes. Sprinkle on the rice (it's important that the black beans are underneath the rice and chicken when the dish goes into the oven, otherwise they get scorched). Pour on the boiling stock and return the chicken to the pan, skin side up. Season.

Bake for 40 minutes. The chicken should be lovely and golden and the stock should have been absorbed. The rice should be tender by this time, too. Sprinkle on the coriander.

Serve with lime wedges, a bowl of pickled chillies, soured cream and slices of avocado (just squeeze lime juice over the avocados in a bowl and sprinkle with salt and pepper).

SERVES 4

FOR THE CHICKEN, BEANS AND RICE

2 tablespoons extra virgin olive oil, or groundnut oil

8 good-sized skin-on bone-in chicken thighs, or a mixture of chicken joints, excess skin neatly trimmed

1 large onion, roughly chopped

2 peppers, halved, deseeded and sliced

3 garlic cloves, finely grated

1 teaspoon ground cumin

1 cinnamon stick, halved

2 red chillies, halved, deseeded and chopped

400g can of black beans, drained and rinsed

150g (5½oz) cherry tomatoes, halved

170g (6oz) basmati rice, washed in a sieve until the water runs clear

600ml (20fl oz) boiling chicken stock

sea salt flakes and freshly ground black pepper

3 tablespoons chopped coriander leaves

TO SERVE
lime wedges
pickled chillies
soured cream
2 avocados

BAKED RICE WITH GREEN OLIVES, ORANGE, FETA CHEESE & DILL

A blueprint for baked rice. Just stick to the same quantities of rice and liquid, the same size of pan and the same oven temperature and you can produce endless variations. Change the herbs, use spices, or add nuts and dried fruit.

Preheat the oven to 190°C fan (400°F), Gas Mark 6.

Wash the rice in a sieve under the cold tap, until the water runs clear, to remove the excess starch, then leave it in the sieve to drain.

In a 30cm (12in) ovenproof sauté pan or shallow casserole, heat the olive oil and sauté the onions over a medium-low heat until they're soft and pale gold. Add the garlic and cumin and cook for another 2 minutes, then add the rinsed and drained rice, orange juice and boiling stock. Season.

Bring to the boil on the hob, then transfer immediately to the oven. Bake, uncovered, for 1 hour.

When there are 10 minutes to go, break up the crust that has formed on the top and stir in the olives. By the end of cooking time, the rice should be tender and all the stock absorbed.

Scatter the orange zest, feta and dill over the top, drizzle with olive oil and serve. You will find that the rice has formed a delicious crust on the base of the pan.

SERVES 8

300g (10½oz) basmati rice

3 tablespoons extra virgin olive oil, plus more to serve

2 large onions, roughly chopped

4 garlic cloves, crushed

1 tablespoon ground cumin

finely grated zest and juice of 1 orange

850ml (1½ pints) boiling chicken or vegetable stock

sea salt flakes and freshly ground black pepper

100g (3½oz) good-quality green olives, preferably pitted, roughly chopped or left whole

150g (5½oz) feta cheese, crumbled

leaves from a small bunch of dill, roughly chopped, any coarse stalks removed

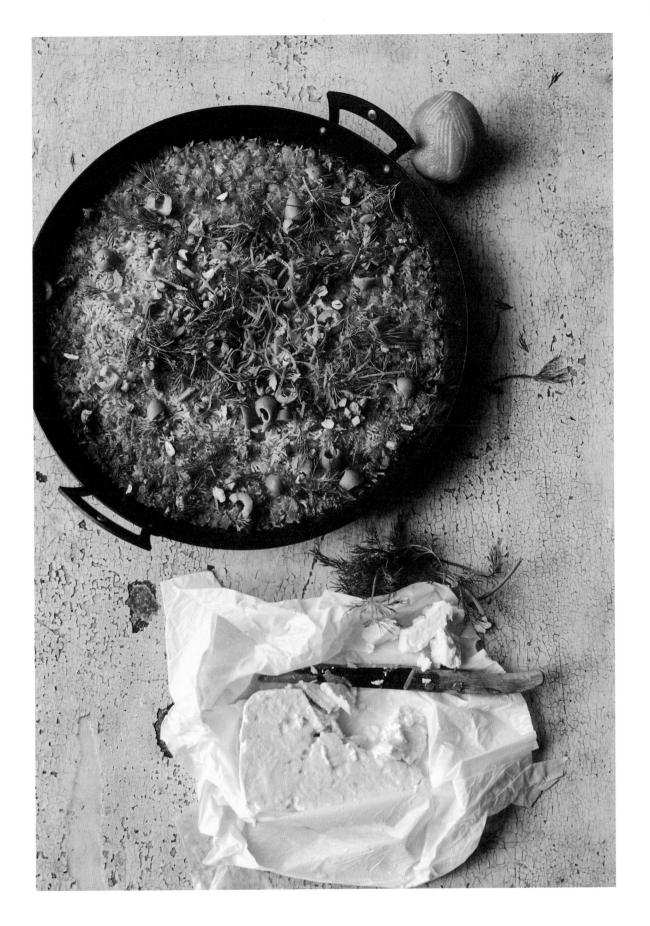

ARROZ AL HORNO

Muscular and comforting, this is brilliant for a cold night. It also feeds eight with very little effort. You do need to use a pan 30–34cm (12–13½in) in diameter, so that the rice cooks at the right rate. Most larger supermarkets stock paella rice now, so it's not difficult to find. Unlike risottos, paellas shouldn't be stirred, which means they're pretty low effort to make.

Preheat the oven to 180°C fan (375°F), Gas Mark 5.

Heat the olive oil in a deep ovenproof frying or sauté pan, or shallow casserole, about 30cm (12in) in diameter, or a little bigger. Over a high heat, colour the pork belly slices on both sides, then lift them out into a bowl.

Reduce the heat to medium, put the black pudding and bacon in the pan and sauté all over, then remove with a slotted spoon and set aside with the pork.

Fry the onion and peppers in the fat remaining in the pan until soft and pale gold, then add the tomato and cook until that is soft, too. Add the garlic, smoked paprika and chilli flakes, if using, and cook for another 2 minutes, then return the pork, black pudding and bacon to the pan. Add the beans, whichever herb you're using and the stock and bring everything to the boil.

Sprinkle the rice around the bits of pork, pushing it below the level of the stock. Return to the boil, season well, then transfer – uncovered – to the oven.

Cook for 30 minutes, without stirring, then check to see how it's doing. The rice should be tender and the stock absorbed. If it's not ready, return it to the oven for another 5 minutes, then check again. Taste for seasoning and adjust it if necessary.

Squeeze lemon juice over the top and drizzle on some extra virgin olive oil, if you want.

SERVES 8

1 tablespoon extra virgin olive oil, plus more to serve (optional)

800g (1lb 12oz) thick boneless pork belly slices (about 4), halved

150g (5½oz) black pudding, chopped

100g (3½oz) chunky unsmoked bacon lardons

1 onion, finely chopped

2 red peppers, halved, deseeded and sliced

1 plum tomato, chopped

8 garlic cloves, roughly chopped

4 teaspoons smoked paprika

½ teaspoon chilli flakes (optional)

½ x 400g can of white beans, drained and rinsed (haricot, cannellini or butter beans are all fine)

6 thyme or rosemary sprigs

1 litre (1¾ pints) chicken stock

375g (13oz) paella rice

sea salt flakes and freshly ground black pepper

lemon juice, to serve (optional)

ARROZ CON VERDURAS

SERVES 6–8

3 tablespoons extra virgin olive oil, plus more to serve (optional)

1 large onion, finely chopped

3 red peppers, halved, deseeded and sliced

6 plum tomatoes, chopped

8 garlic cloves, roughly chopped

5 teaspoons smoked paprika, or less, if you prefer

½ teaspoon chilli flakes

400g can of chickpeas, drained and rinsed

6 thyme sprigs

1.5 litres (2½ pints) vegetable stock, plus more if needed

generous pinch of saffron threads (optional)

350g (12oz) paella rice

600g (1lb 5oz) pumpkin or squash, seeds and fibres removed, cut into wedges

sea salt flakes and freshly ground black pepper

115g (4oz) purple sprouting broccoli, any thicker stems halved lengthways

lemon juice, to serve (optional)

You can use any vegetables you like here – tomatoes, pumpkin, aubergines, courgettes, whatever is in season – just make sure that anything that takes a long time to cook is cut small enough to be ready in the time the dish is in the oven. Conversely, quick-cooking vegetables such as broccoli or asparagus should be added to the dish later on. This is quite spicy; if you want a milder version, reduce the quantities of smoked paprika and chilli. Allioli – garlic mayonnaise – is lovely with this, if you can be bothered to make it (see page 198).

Preheat the oven to 190°C fan (400°F), Gas Mark 6.

Heat 2 tablespoons of the olive oil in a shallow casserole or a large ovenproof sauté pan, or a paella pan measuring around 30cm (12in) in diameter (a little bigger or smaller is OK).

Fry the onion and peppers until soft and pale gold, then add the tomatoes and cook until they are soft too, and the mixture is thick and sloppy.

Add the garlic, smoked paprika and chilli flakes and cook for 2 minutes. Stir in the chickpeas, thyme, stock and saffron (if you're using it) and bring to the boil. Sprinkle the rice on top and lay the pumpkin slices in the pan.

Season well and transfer the dish to the oven, uncovered. Cook for 25 minutes without stirring, then check to see how the rice is doing. It should be almost tender and the stock nearly absorbed. If the stock has already been absorbed and there is a danger of the rice drying out, pour in a little more.

Toss the broccoli in the remaining 1 tablespoon oil, season and scatter it over the top. Return to the oven for a final 10 minutes.

Squeeze some lemon juice over the dish, if you like, and serve, drizzled with some extra virgin olive oil, if you want.

CHICKEN & RICE WITH COCONUT, GREEN CHILLIES, CORIANDER & LIME

SERVES 4–6

1 tbsp groundnut oil

8 good-sized skin-on bone-in chicken thighs, excess skin neatly trimmed

1 large onion, roughly chopped

4 garlic cloves, finely grated

3cm (1¼in) fresh root ginger, peeled and finely grated

2 teaspoons ground coriander

2 teaspoons ground cumin

2 green chillies, halved, deseeded and finely chopped

200g (7oz) butternut squash, peeled, deseeded and sliced (prepared weight)

100g (3½oz) cauliflower florets

225g (8oz) basmati rice

leaves from 25g (scant 1oz) bunch of coriander, chopped

finely grated zest and juice of 2 limes

2 lime leaves

sea salt flakes and freshly ground black pepper

300ml (½ pint) coconut milk

400ml (14fl oz) chicken stock

chutney and natural yogurt, to serve (optional)

Easy one-dish cooking. Leave the seeds of one of the chillies intact if you prefer things hotter. You can use just a single vegetable (cauliflower or squash) instead of both, if you like. You don't have to serve any more vegetables on the side, but some chutney and yogurt would be good.

Preheat the oven to 180°C fan (375°F), Gas Mark 5.

Heat the oil in a shallow casserole or sauté pan, 30cm (12in) in diameter, and quickly fry the chicken thighs just to get some colour on them (they will darken further in the oven). Remove them and put them on a plate.

Sauté the onion in the pan until it's soft and pale gold. Add the garlic, ginger, the spices and chillies and cook for 2 minutes, then stir in the squash and cauliflower. Tip in the rice, half the coriander, the lime zest, half the lime juice, the lime leaves and seasoning. Return the chicken to the pan skin side up, along with any juices that have run from it. Season the top of the chicken.

Heat the coconut milk and chicken stock in a saucepan until just under boiling. Pour this around the chicken thighs and put the pan into the oven, uncovered. Cook for 35 minutes. The chicken should be cooked through and the liquid should have been absorbed by the rice.

Squeeze the remaining lime juice over the top and scatter with the rest of the coriander. Serve immediately, with chutney and yogurt, if you like.

CHICKEN WITH WILD MUSHROOMS, PUMPKIN, RICE & SAGE BUTTER

If the butter is an effort too far, leave it out, it's still a good dish. This is also lovely with a generous handful of grated Parmesan or pecorino cheese sprinkled on top 15 minutes before the end of the cooking time. You don't have to use only chicken thighs, you can use a mixture of thighs and drumsticks, if you prefer.

Preheat the oven to 190°C fan (400°F), Gas Mark 6.

Soak the wild mushrooms in 75ml (2½fl oz) just-boiled water for 15 minutes.

To make the sage butter, mash the butter with the sage and garlic and set it aside (I only chill this if I'm going to keep it for a while).

Drain the wild mushrooms, adding their soaking liquid to the chicken stock.

Wash the rice in a sieve under the cold tap, until the water runs clear, to remove the excess starch.

Put the onion and both the chestnut and dried mushrooms into a 30cm (12in) sauté pan or shallow casserole (the width is very important) and sprinkle on the rice (it may not look like much, but it expands, don't worry). Put the chicken thighs, skin side up, and the pumpkin on top. Sprinkle a little olive oil over the vegetables and chicken and season well. Bring the stock mixture to the boil, then carefully pour it around the chicken thighs.

Bake in the oven for 45 minutes, by which time the chicken will be lovely and golden and the stock will have been absorbed. Put knobs of the sage butter over the chicken thighs, allow it to melt, then serve.

FOR THE CHICKEN AND RICE

15g (½oz) dried wild mushrooms

500ml (18fl oz) chicken stock

170g (6oz) basmati rice

1 onion, roughly chopped

125g (4½oz) chestnut mushrooms, trimmed and thickly sliced

8 good-sized skin-on bone-in chicken thighs, excess skin neatly trimmed

345g (12oz) pumpkin or butternut squash, deseeded and chopped into big chunks or wedges (prepared weight)

a little extra virgin olive oil

sea salt flakes and freshly ground black pepper

FOR THE SAGE BUTTER

75g (2¾oz) unsalted butter, at room temperature

6 sage leaves, finely chopped

1 small garlic clove, finely grated

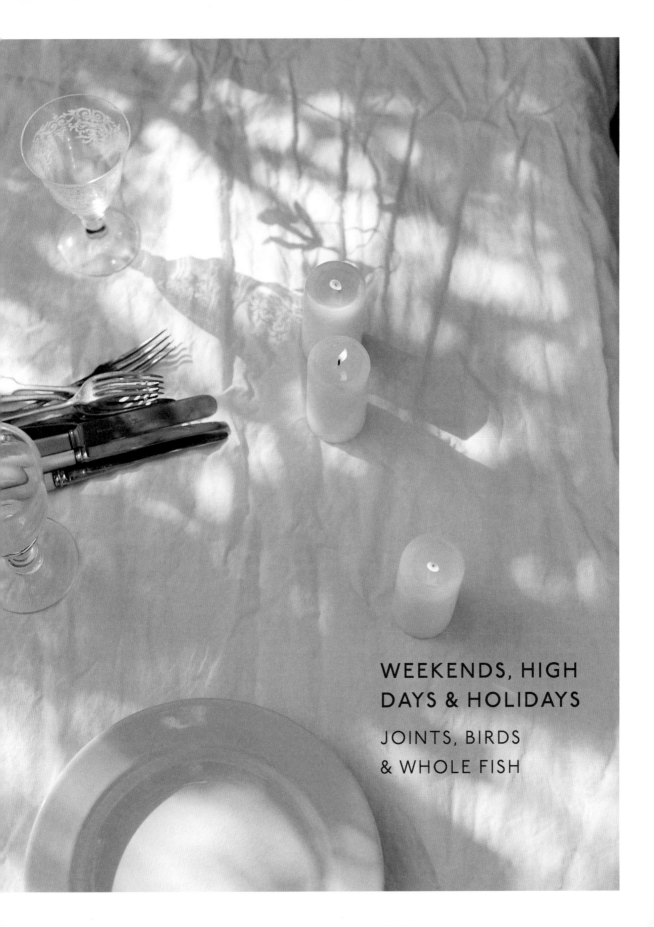

WEEKENDS, HIGH DAYS & HOLIDAYS

JOINTS, BIRDS & WHOLE FISH

HOT & SWEET GINGER POUSSINS

Sticky, messy, quick. I sometimes split the poussins, to make them easier for people to deal with (children can find them hard to tackle, though using your hands should be encouraged). In the summer, a cucumber salad is good alongside (see page 184); in the winter, stir-fried pak choi. Provide plenty of paper napkins.

Put the *kecap manis*, soy sauce and fish sauce in a saucepan with the sugar. Heat gently, stirring to help the sugar dissolve. Leave to cool, then add the lime juice, sriracha, garlic and ginger.

Place the poussins into a dish and add the marinade, making sure it goes inside the birds' cavities as well as over the outsides. Cover the dish with cling film and put in the fridge, preferably overnight, but even for a couple of hours is good. Turn the birds over in the marinade every so often. When you're ready to cook, bring the birds to room temperature.

Preheat the oven to 180°C fan (375°F), Gas Mark 5.

Put the poussins into a roasting tin – or 2 roasting tins if yours are small – and roast for 50 minutes.

Pour the marinade left behind into a small saucepan and bring to the boil, then remove from the heat. Use this to baste the poussins as they cook (it's very important to reheat the marinade to boiling point, so it's safe for you to use it to baste the part-cooked birds).

You might have to cover the poussins with foil towards the end of the cooking time. They'll become a lovely dark mahogany colour, but you don't want them to burn. To test for doneness, check the juices that run from between the body of a bird and the leg when it is pierced are clear, with no trace of pink.

Serve the poussins brushed with a final layer of the marinade and sprinkled with sesame seeds. These are good with boiled rice, a stir-fried green vegetable such as pak choi and lime wedges.

SERVES 6

FOR THE POUSSINS
250ml (9fl oz) *kecap manis* (Indonesian sweet soy sauce)

125ml (4fl oz) light soy sauce

125ml (4fl oz) fish sauce

115g (4oz) soft light brown sugar

juice of 2 limes

2 tablespoons sriracha, plus more if you want the poussins to be hotter

4 garlic cloves, finely grated

4cm (1½in) fresh root ginger, peeled and finely grated

6 poussins

TO SERVE
sesame seeds

boiled rice

stir-fried green vegetables

lime wedges

SALMON ROASTED IN BUTTER WITH BEETROOT & HORSERADISH PURÉE

A whole salmon can seem like a real number – we faff about with fish kettles and the like – and, even when roasted, it is a big thing to eat your way through. A side of salmon cooked in butter, however, is less expensive and serves a smaller number of people, but still has impact. If you don't like beetroot, serve another sauce; a mixture of mayonnaise and fromage frais with chopped herbs, capers and shallots is good, or check the endless list of possible embellishments (see pages 206–207).

Preheat the oven to 220°C fan (450°F), Gas Mark 8.

For the purée, put everything except the crème fraîche into a food processor, season and whizz until smooth. Scrape this into a bowl and add the crème fraîche. Taste for seasoning. You might need to adjust the lemon juice and vinegar, too.

Find a heavy roasting tin big enough to take the side of salmon. Run your hand over the surface of the fish from head to tail to make sure that there are no bones; if there are, remove them. Season the fish.

Melt the butter in the tin over a medium-low heat on the hob, then add half the herbs and put the salmon on top, skin side up. Transfer to the oven and roast for 5 minutes. Remove from the oven and take the skin off – it should peel off quite easily – then season the flesh and flip the salmon over. Sprinkle with the remaining herbs and return to the oven for a final 6–8 minutes. Carefully slide the point of a sharp knife into the thickest part of the fish: it should not be glassy.

Serve on a warmed platter with dill (or chervil) sprigs and lemon wedges. Offer the beetroot and horseradish purée on the side.

FOR THE PURÉE

400g (14oz) cooked beetroot (not pickled)

1 small garlic clove, finely grated

juice of ½ lemon, or to taste

1 tablespoon white balsamic vinegar, or to taste

1 tablespoon peeled and finely grated fresh horseradish

1 tablespoon crème fraîche

sea salt flakes and freshly ground black pepper

FOR THE FISH

1kg (2lb 4oz) side of salmon, filleted and pin-boned

50g (1¾oz) unsalted butter

3 tablespoons chopped mixed flat leaf parsley and dill leaves (chervil is also fantastic, if you can find it or you grow it), plus dill sprigs to serve

lemon wedges, to serve

ROAST LEG OF LAMB WITH BASIL, PECORINO, GARLIC & WINE

This came about after I cooked a Greek dish that had a stuffing made from a Greek cheese (not unlike pecorino) and ground allspice. I'd never thought about a cheese stuffing for lamb before. So this is just something that came out of my kitchen for Sunday lunch one week: Italian ingredients, Greek-inspired.

Preheat the oven to 220°C fan (450°F), Gas Mark 8.

Put the cheese, garlic and some salt into a mortar and pound to a rough purée, gradually adding the olive oil. Tear the basil leaves, add them to the mortar and pound them, too.

Place the leg of lamb in a roasting tin. Make deep incisions all over it and push the paste from the mortar down into them. You can also loosen the meat around the bone to make a pocket and push the paste into that, too. Season all over and put into the oven.

Roast for 15 minutes, then reduce the oven temperature to 180°C fan (375°F), Gas Mark 5. Add the onions, potatoes and tomatoes to the roasting tin, toss them in the fat in the pan, adding a little more oil if it's needed to moisten them, then season and roast for a final 45 minutes, adding the wine after 20 minutes. The lamb will be pink. If you prefer it more well done, cook it for a little longer.

Remove the lamb to a plate, cover with foil, insulate well (I use old towels or tea towels) and leave to rest for 15 minutes. If the potatoes are tender, cover them and keep warm in a low oven while the lamb rests; if they're still a bit firm, increase the oven temperature to 200°C fan (410°F), Gas Mark 6½, return the vegetables to the oven, uncovered, and cook until they're ready.

Serve the lamb with the potatoes, tomatoes and onions, scattered with a few basil leaves, if you like.

SERVES 6–8

120g (4¼oz) pecorino cheese, finely grated

6 garlic cloves, finely grated

sea salt flakes and freshly ground black pepper

3 tablespoons extra virgin olive oil, plus more if needed

leaves from a small bunch of basil, plus more to serve (optional)

1.8kg (4lb) leg of lamb

2 medium red onions, cut into wedges

600g (1lb 5oz) small waxy potatoes, scrubbed, then halved or quartered, depending on size

350g (12oz) red and yellow tomatoes, halved or quartered

250ml (9fl oz) white wine

PERSIAN-SPICED SPATCHCOCKED CHICKEN WITH QUICK-PICKLED RED ONIONS & DILL YOGURT

The recipe for the spice mix here makes more than you need, but keep it for next time. You can obviously leave out the pickled red onions if you want, but the spice mix is quite aromatic, so they bring a good tart-sweet contrast.

To make the spice mix, put the peppercorns, coriander seeds, cardamom seeds and rose petals, if using, into a mortar and bash until roughly ground. Add the nutmeg and turmeric.

Spatchcock the chicken (it's easy, *see* page 198). Put it in a large roasting tin.

Mix 4 of the garlic cloves with the 2 tablespoons olive oil and some seasoning. Carefully lift the skin on the chicken breast and, without tearing it, loosen it so that you can push the garlic and oil paste over the breast and, if you can lift the skin enough, on to the legs.

Rub 1 tablespoon of the spice mix all over the bird and season. Smear with olive oil and rub that in, too. Cover and put it into the fridge to marinate for up to 6 hours, or you can roast it straight away. If you're cooking it now, preheat the oven to 190°C fan (400°F), Gas Mark 6. Roast for 1 hour.

For the quick-pickled onions, heat the vinegar with 5 tablespoons water, the sugar and a pinch of sea salt flakes until the sugar and salt dissolve. Add the onion and remove from the heat. Leave to sit for 1 hour (longer is fine).

Stir the reserved grated garlic clove into the yogurt with the dill. Serve the chicken with the pickled onions, yogurt and a bowl of rice or bulgur wheat.

SERVES 6

FOR THE SPICE MIX
1 tablespoon black peppercorns

1 teaspoon coriander seeds

seeds from 8 cardamom pods

1 tablespoon dried rose petals (optional)

½ teaspoon freshly grated nutmeg

¾ teaspoon ground turmeric

FOR THE CHICKEN
1.8kg (4lb) chicken

5 garlic cloves, finely grated

2 tablespoons extra virgin olive oil, plus more to rub

sea salt flakes and freshly ground black pepper

300g (10½oz) Greek yogurt

20g (¾oz) bunch of dill, leaves chopped, any coarse stalks discarded

rice or bulgur wheat, to serve

FOR THE QUICK-PICKLED ONIONS
100ml (3½fl oz) white wine vinegar

50g (1¾oz) granulated sugar

1 red onion, finely sliced

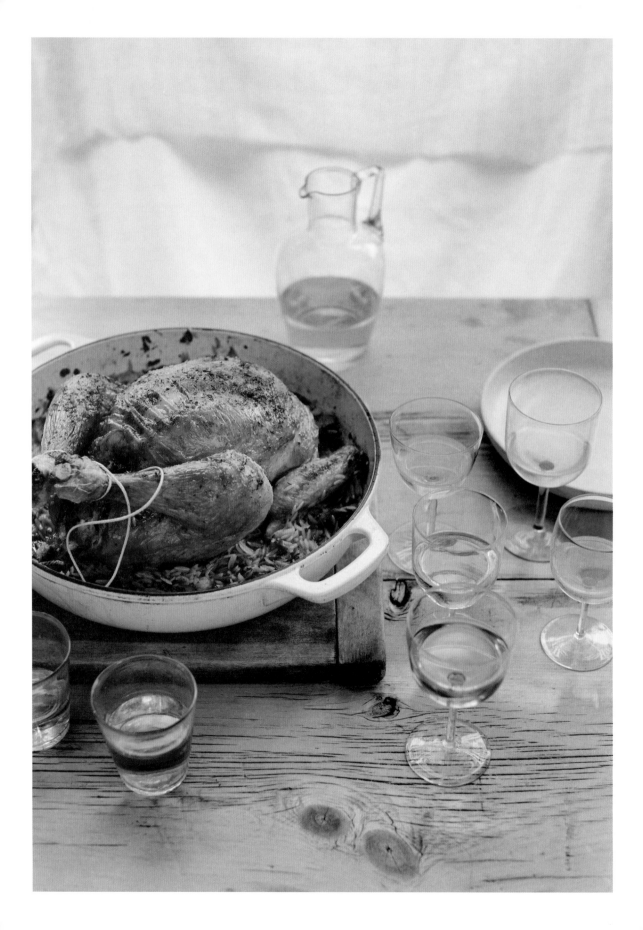

STUFFED GREEK CHICKEN WITH CAYENNE, OREGANO & ORZO

The perfect recipe for a spring Sunday lunch, with everything you need all in one dish. You have double carbs – orzo and stuffing – but it works: the bread becomes deliciously soft and soggy with the juices from the tomatoes. Try serving it with Roast radishes with honey, mint & preserved lemon (see page 73), open some rosé and contemplate the approaching summer.

Preheat the oven to 190°C fan (400°F), Gas Mark 6.

Put the chicken into an ovenproof dish – I use a cast iron one – which is 30cm (12in) in diameter. Mix the feta, tomatoes, bread, olive oil, garlic, half the dried oregano and some seasoning in a bowl. Stuff this into the chicken cavity.

Rub the chicken – breast and legs – with the cayenne, sprinkle with the rest of the dried oregano, then season the bird and drizzle it with olive oil.

Roast in the oven for 50 minutes.

Sprinkle the orzo around the chicken and pour on the boiling stock. Return to the oven for a final 20 minutes. Check during this time to make sure the orzo isn't becoming dry: there should be enough stock in it, but top it up with a little boiling water if you need to.

The chicken should be cooked: check by piercing it deeply between the leg and the body, the juices that run out should be clear, with no traces of pink. The orzo should be tender and the stock should have been absorbed.

Stir the fresh chopped herbs into the orzo and serve the chicken straight from the dish. A green salad or roasted red peppers is all you need on the side.

SERVES 6

1.8kg (4lb) chicken

75g (2¾oz) feta cheese, crumbled

115g (4oz) tomatoes, chopped

75g (2¾oz) coarse country bread, torn into small pieces

4 tablespoons extra virgin olive oil, plus more to drizzle

2 garlic cloves, finely grated

3 teaspoons dried oregano

sea salt flakes and freshly ground black pepper

½ teaspoon cayenne pepper

225g (8oz) orzo

500ml (18fl oz) boiling chicken stock

1 tablespoon chopped flat leaf parsley leaves, or chopped leaves from 4 oregano sprigs

green salad, or roasted peppers, to serve

ROAST PORK WITH CRUSHED GRAPES, MARSALA & JUNIPER

I don't cook roast pork that often – I just didn't grow up with it, we were a lamb- and chicken-eating family – but when I do, it's usually with fruit. This is gorgeously autumnal.

Unroll the pork and lay it on a board, flesh side up. Make incisions all over the meat with a sharp knife, then push the slivers of garlic into the incisions.

Crush the salt, peppercorns, rosemary leaves and juniper berries roughly in a mortar, then stir in the olive oil.

Rub the seasoning mix into the pork, again on the flesh side, pushing bits inside the incisions. Put in a dish, cover and refrigerate overnight.

The next day, remove the pork from the fridge and allow it to come to room temperature. Preheat the oven to 200°C fan (410°F), Gas Mark 6½.

Roll the loin firmly, keeping as much of the seasoning inside as you can, then tie it at intervals with kitchen string. Put it in a heavy roasting tin and season all over. Roast for 25 minutes, then reduce the oven temperature to 180°C fan (375°F), Gas Mark 5.

Pull half the grapes from their stems, cut the rest of the bunch into sprigs, and add them all to the roasting tin with 250ml (9fl oz) of the Marsala. Continue roasting for 60 minutes. Test the meat for doneness: the juices should run clear when the flesh is pierced to the centre with a metal skewer.

Remove the pork from the tin, along with the grapes that are on sprigs, and put them on a warmed serving platter. Cover and allow to rest for 15 minutes.

Set the roasting tin over a medium heat, add the remaining Marsala and crush the loose grapes into the juices. Boil until you have a slightly syrupy mixture. Serve the pork with the Marsala sauce and the sprigs of roasted grapes.

1.8kg (4lb) boned pork loin, scored

6 garlic cloves, cut into fine slivers

½ tablespoon sea salt flakes

½ tablespoon black peppercorns

leaves from 3 rosemary sprigs

1 tablespoon juniper berries

2 tablespoons extra virgin olive oil

500g (1lb 2oz) black seedless grapes

350ml (12fl oz) dry Marsala

ROAST FILLET OF BEEF WITH CRIMSON LEAVES, BUTTERMILK, WALNUTS & CASHEL BLUE CHEESE

A very expensive dish, I know, but this is the kind of thing to serve on festive occasions such as Thanksgiving, Christmas or New Year. It's particularly good on those days that aren't weighed down by a traditional dish (basically, when you don't have to serve a turkey), but you want something luxurious and generous. I wouldn't serve a roasted vegetable as well, just some boiled little waxy potatoes or good bread.

Preheat the oven to 210°C fan (425°F), Gas Mark 7.

Bring the meat to room temperature. Season the beef really well all over and heat the oil or dripping in a large frying pan. When the fat is smoking, add the beef and colour it on all sides. Transfer the joint to a roasting tin and roast for 10 minutes, then reduce the oven temperature to 190°C fan (400°F), Gas Mark 6 and cook for another 20 minutes. Cover the meat with foil, insulate it with tea towels or old towels and leave it to rest for 15 minutes.

To make the dressing, put the buttermilk, soured cream, olive oil, white balsamic vinegar, mustard, garlic and seasoning into a bowl and mix with a fork. Taste for seasoning.

Put the leaves – tear the larger ones – into a broad shallow bowl or on to a platter and throw on the walnuts and the cheese. Drizzle or spoon the dressing over the top (don't drown the leaves, just serve the extra dressing on the side).

Slice the beef and serve it with the leaves, cheese and dressing.

SERVES 8

FOR THE BEEF

1.8kg (4lb) fillet of beef

sea salt flakes and freshly ground black pepper

1 tablespoon groundnut oil, or beef dripping

FOR THE SALAD

250ml (9fl oz) buttermilk

3 tablespoons soured cream

2 tablespoons extra virgin olive oil

2 tablespoons white balsamic vinegar

1 teaspoon Dijon mustard

1 small garlic clove, finely grated

400g (14oz) bitter crimson leaves, a mixture of Treviso tardive (the one that looks like purple quills), radicchio and red chicory is ideal

75g (2¾oz) walnuts, lightly toasted

150g (5½oz) Cashel Blue cheese, crumbled

TAMARIND MACKEREL WITH MANGO, LIME & CHILLI SALAD

People are divided about mackerel and most don't view it positively, partly because it's strong, very much itself. It's impossible to mute mackerel, but its oiliness is brilliant with chilli, rhubarb, ginger, turmeric, tamarind... all the flavours that more subtle ingredients end up fighting with. You can serve the fish with rice, but they're also excellent with bread (mackerel are served stuffed into bread in Istanbul, as street food). Get your guests to remove the flesh, stuff it into warm naan with the mango salad, daub it with yogurt and eat. Mackerel's unarguable-with quality is precisely what makes this work.

Mix together the garlic, ginger and all the spices for the mackerel, adding the lime juice, sugar, oil and seasoning. Spread this all over each fish, inside and out. Cover and put in the fridge for about 15 minutes.

Preheat the oven to 200°C fan (410°F), Gas Mark 6½.

Now make the salad. Peel the mangoes and cut off the 'cheeks' (the fleshy bits that lie alongside the stone). Cut the cheeks into neat slices. (Use the rest of the flesh from the mangoes for something else... or eat it.)

Put the mango slices in a serving bowl and add the lime juice, chillies, some salt and the coriander and toss.

Put some foil or greaseproof paper in a roasting tin and put the mackerel into it. Roast the mackerel for 20 minutes (if the fish are very big, they might need a little longer; make sure the flesh near the bone is opaque, not glassy).

Squeeze some lime juice over the fish and serve with rice, or warmed naan bread and yogurt, lime wedges and the mango and chilli salad.

SERVES 4

FOR THE FISH

2 garlic cloves, finely grated

4cm (1½in) fresh root ginger, peeled and finely grated

¾ teaspoon ground turmeric

1½ teaspoons ground cumin

½ teaspoon ground fenugreek

2½ tablespoons tamarind paste

4 tablespoons lime juice, plus more to serve, plus lime wedges to serve

1 tablespoon soft light brown sugar

2 tablespoons groundnut oil

sea salt flakes and freshly ground black pepper

4 whole mackerel, gutted and washed

rice, or warmed naan bread and natural yogurt, to serve

FOR THE SALAD

2 just-ripe or slightly under-ripe mangoes

juice of 2 limes

1 red chilli and 1 green chilli, halved, deseeded and very finely shredded

10g (¼oz) coriander leaves and stalks (make sure the stalks aren't too long or coarse)

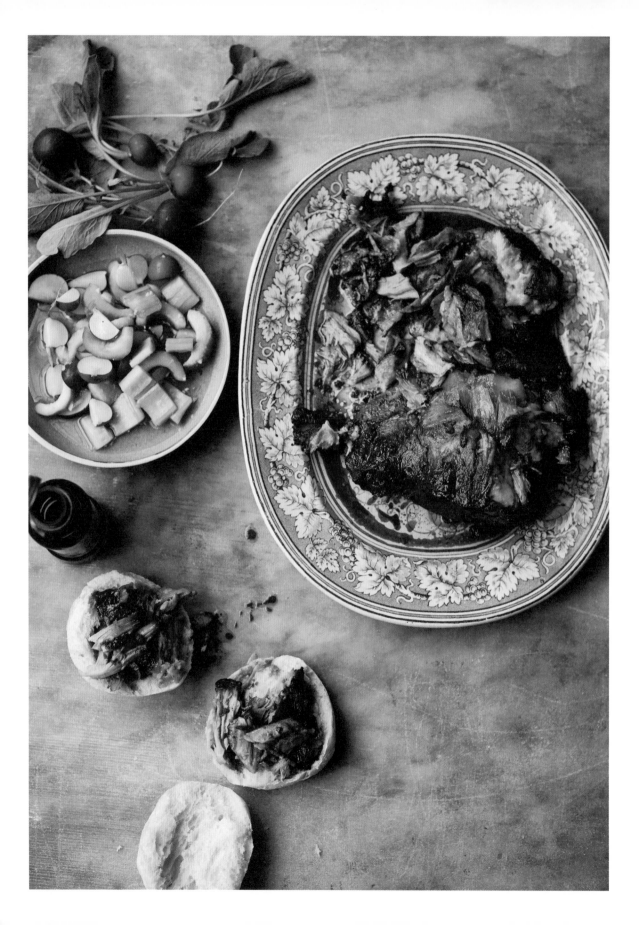

SERVES 6

FOR THE PORK

1.9kg (4lb 4oz) boned pork
shoulder

125ml (4fl oz) soy sauce

125ml (4fl oz) runny honey

125ml (4fl oz) hoisin sauce

125ml (4fl oz) amontillado
sherry

2 teaspoons five spice

3cm (1¼in) fresh root
ginger, peeled and
finely grated

TO SERVE

boiled rice, or soft white
bread rolls

Radish & cucumber salad
(see overleaf), to serve

crisp lettuce leaves

SLOW-ROAST HOISIN PORK SHOULDER
WITH RADISH & CUCUMBER SALAD

*It's really important to get excellent pork for this. A joint from the
supermarket won't be good enough, either in flavour or texture.
Go to your butcher. Apart from basting the meat for the last hour
of cooking, this is pretty hassle-free.*

Remove the skin from the pork – or ask your butcher to do it for you – and
discard. Leave the fat on.

Mix together all the other ingredients for the pork in a small bowl to make
a marinade. Put this in a large plastic food bag, if possible, or a roasting tin,
with the pork. Marinate in the fridge for 24–48 hours.

Bring the pork to room temperature by removing it from the fridge for at least
1 hour before you are going to cook it.

Preheat the oven to 130°C fan (275°F), Gas Mark 1.

Put the pork into a roasting tin in which it will fit snugly (if there is a lot of
room around it, the juices and the marinade will just run off and burn) and
pour the marinade into a saucepan. Roast the pork for 4½–5 hours, or until
the meat is soft and melting. Bring the marinade to the boil, then remove
from the heat (it's very important to reheat the marinade to boiling point,
so it's safe for you to use it to baste the part-cooked pork).

Now ladle some of the marinade over the pork and return to the oven. Keep
adding more of the marinade and basting the pork every 10 minutes for the
next hour. Turn it over every time you do this. The pork should end up dark
and glossy. If the joint starts to get too dark on the outside, cover it with foil.

continued >

FOR THE SALAD

3 tablespoons rice vinegar

3 teaspoons caster sugar

pinch of fine sea salt

2cm (¾in) fresh root ginger, peeled and finely grated

1 large garlic clove, very finely chopped or grated

1 cucumber, chilled

300g (10½oz) radishes (a mixture of colours if possible), quartered, or cut into eighths if they're big

1 teaspoon toasted sesame oil

1 teaspoon toasted sesame seeds (a mixture of white and black, if you like)

To make the salad, mix the vinegar, sugar, salt, ginger and garlic together. Peel the cucumber in stripes. Halve it along its length and scoop out the seeds, then cut it into 4cm (1½in) lengths. Bash these with a mallet or a rolling pin. Put the cucumber into a serving bowl with the dressing and place in the fridge for 20 minutes. When you're ready to eat, add the radishes and the sesame oil and toss everything together. Scatter the sesame seeds on top.

Serve the pork with boiled rice, or in soft white bread rolls, with the radish and cucumber salad, and with crisp lettuce leaves.

VON DIAZ'S SWEET & SOUR CHICKEN & CHORIZO IN ADOBO

As soon as I cooked this, it went straight into my core repertoire of oft-repeated dishes. It's from Coconuts & Collards *by American food writer Von Diaz, a book about combining Puerto Rican food (Von was born there) with the food of the American South, where she grew up. The chicken becomes melting and smoky. I've changed Von's recipe a little – adding more liquid and chorizo – with her approval, and adapted it so it can be cooked in the oven rather than on the hob; it works either way, though the timings are different.*

Put the chicken into a dish or a large plastic food bag. In a bowl, mix the garlic, oregano, salt, pepper, olive oil and lemon juice and rub this inside the chicken as well as outside. Cover the dish, or seal the bag, and leave in the fridge overnight, or for at least 1 hour. Bring it to room temperature.

Preheat the oven to 200°C fan (410°F), Gas Mark 6½.

Scrape the marinade off the outside of the bird (or the oregano and garlic will burn) and heat the butter in a casserole big enough for the chicken. Brown the chicken, breast side down first, then on the other sides, being careful not to burn it. Take it out and add the sausages to the pan. Brown them all over, then add the sugar and vinegar. Bring to the boil, stirring to help the sugar dissolve, then reduce the heat to low. Push the sausages to the edges of the pan and put the chicken in the middle, breast side down.

Transfer to the oven and cook for 20 minutes. Reduce the oven temperature to 180°C fan (375°F), Gas Mark 5, cover and cook for a further 30 minutes. Spoon the juices up over the bird, turn it breast side up, and roast for a final 15 minutes, uncovered. Check for doneness by piercing the bird between the leg and body: the juices that run out should be clear, with no trace of pink.

Slice the sausages and give everyone some sausage, some chicken and plenty of the cooking juices. This really calls for boiled rice on the side.

SERVES 6

1.8kg (4lb) chicken

10 garlic cloves, finely grated

2 tablespoons dried oregano

1 tablespoon sea salt flakes and lots of freshly ground black pepper

4 tablespoons extra virgin olive oil

juice of 2 lemons

50g (1¾oz) unsalted butter

6 chorizo cooking sausages

100g (3½oz) soft light brown sugar

100ml (3½fl oz) red wine vinegar

boiled rice, to serve

BAKED SEA BASS WITH RAISINS, PRESERVED LEMONS, GINGER & CORIANDER

This was inspired by a salmon dish cooked by the late George Perry-Smith many moons ago in The Hole in the Wall restaurant in Bath. His recipe is stuffed with ginger, almonds and raisins, wrapped in pastry and served with a herb sauce: sauce messine. It has always seemed very medieval to me, its stuffing Arab-influenced. I still make his dish – and love it – but it takes a bit of work and is very rich. This uses similar flavours and ingredients, with the addition of preserved lemons, but is much simpler. You could also use a whole salmon instead of sea bass.

Preheat the oven to 210°C fan (425°F), Gas Mark 7. Make the spice paste by mixing everything together in a bowl. Make the stuffing in the same way in a separate bowl, adding plenty of seasoning to both mixtures.

Wash the fish to get rid of any blood (it's bitter) and pat dry with kitchen paper. Put a double layer of greaseproof paper into a roasting tray or tin big enough for the fish. Brush the centre – where the fish will lie – with olive oil.

Make diagonal slashes in the fish on each side, cutting down to the bone but not through it. Push the spice paste inside the slits on both sides. Carefully stuff the butter mixture inside the fish, pushing it up into the head to get all of it in (you're not going to eat the head, but you will be able to get the stuffing out of it). Put the fish on to the oiled greaseproof paper. Lay the lemon slices inside and on top, then drizzle with olive oil and season.

Bake for 30 minutes, then check for doneness: the flesh near the bone in the thickest part of the fish should be white, not glassy. If it needs a little longer, return it to the oven for no more than a couple of minutes, then check again.

Serve with lemon wedges and a bowl of couscous tossed with some chopped pistachios, lemon juice and finely grated lemon zest.

FOR THE SPICE PASTE

20g (¾oz) fresh root ginger, peeled and finely grated

2 garlic cloves, finely grated

scant ¼ teaspoon cayenne pepper

juice of ½ small lemon

2 tablespoons extra virgin olive oil

sea salt flakes and freshly ground black pepper

FOR THE STUFFING

125g (4½oz) unsalted butter, softened

40g (1½oz) ground almonds

75g (2¾oz) raisins, soaked in boiling water for 15 minutes, then drained and patted dry

2 globes of stem ginger, very finely chopped

2 preserved lemons, flesh and rind finely chopped, pips removed

1 garlic clove, finely grated

2 tablespoons chopped coriander leaves

FOR THE FISH

1.9kg (4lb 4oz) sea bass, gutted, scaled and washed

a little extra virgin olive oil

1 unwaxed lemon, finely sliced, plus lemon wedges to serve

couscous, to serve

SLOW-COOKED LEG OF LAMB WITH SHERRY & AUTUMN VEGETABLES

SERVES 8

8 garlic cloves, plus 1 head of garlic, cloves separated

sea salt flakes and freshly ground black pepper

large pinch of saffron threads (optional)

leaves from 8 thyme sprigs, plus 4 whole thyme sprigs

8 tablespoons extra virgin olive oil

2kg (4lb 8oz) leg of lamb

1 large onion, cut into wedges

300g (10½oz) slim bunched carrots, or, if you can only find fatter carrots, halve or quarter them lengthways

500g (1lb 2oz) waxy potatoes, scrubbed and sliced (no need to peel)

400ml (14fl oz) amontillado sherry, plus more if needed

Of course the lamb is supposed to be the star here, but the vegetables are a revelation. They soak up the lamb juices as they cook, becoming really imbued with the flavour both of the lamb and of the sherry. You have all you need in one dish here, but if you want something green, make Olive oil-roast sweet & sour leaves with raisins and pine nuts (see page 117).

Preheat the oven to 220°C fan (450°F), Gas Mark 8.

Crush the 8 cloves of garlic in a mortar and pestle with some sea salt flakes (the salt flakes act as an abrasive). Grind in the saffron, if using; it will add its flavour, and of course its gorgeous colour, but the dish is just as delicious without. Add the thyme leaves, pepper and olive oil, to give a loose paste.

Make incisions all over the lamb with a knife and slightly loosen the meat around the bone end, too. Push the garlic and herb paste down into these incisions, into the space around the bone and all over the joint. Put into a large roasting tin or a cast iron casserole; you will need to add all the vegetables later, too, so there has to be room for them as well. Season all over.

Roast for 20 minutes, then remove the tin or casserole from the oven. Reduce the oven temperature to 160°C fan (340°F), Gas Mark 3½. Put the onion, carrots, the rest of the garlic cloves, potatoes and thyme sprigs under and around the lamb. Bring the sherry to just under the boil, then pour it over. Cover tightly with a double layer of foil, or the lid, and return to the oven.

Cook for 2½ hours, turning the lamb over about 3 times and checking on the sherry, too: most of it will be absorbed during cooking, but don't let it get dry. If there are a lot of juices, remove the foil or uncover the pot 45 minutes before the end of cooking time, so they can reduce. The lamb should be cooked to softness – if it isn't, cook it for a little longer – and the vegetables completely tender. Serve the lamb with the vegetables and the sherry juices.

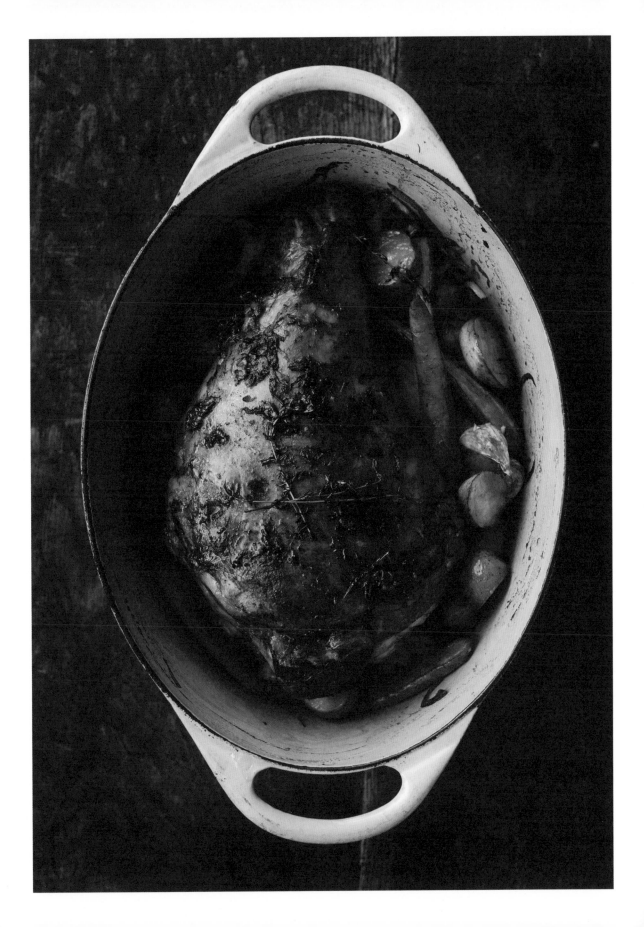

SERVES 6

FOR THE SALSA VERDE

1 unwaxed lemon (not too small), cut into 6 slices, each about 3mm (⅛in) thick

150ml (5fl oz) extra virgin olive oil

10 anchovies, drained of oil

15 basil leaves

15 mint leaves

leaves from a small bunch of flat leaf parsley

¼ tablespoon Dijon mustard

1 garlic clove, chopped

1 tablespoon capers, rinsed, drained and patted dry

FOR THE FISH

5 tablespoons extra virgin olive oil

sea salt flakes and freshly ground black pepper

1.5kg (3lb 5oz) monkfish tail on the bone, skinned and membrane removed

3 garlic cloves, finely sliced

leaves from 4 rosemary sprigs

GIGOT OF MONKFISH WITH ROAST LEMON SALSA VERDE

This is an expensive dish, but it's a huge treat; one for your best, most appreciative friends. It's called a gigot because the shape of a monkfish tail is like that of a leg of lamb. I love the lemon in the salsa verde, but there are lots of other sauces in the book that would work with this, too: have a look at the Roast pepper, caper and preserved lemon relish (see page 207).

Preheat the oven to 150°C fan (325°F), Gas Mark 3.

Put the lemon slices for the salsa verde on to a baking tray lined with baking parchment. Cook for 25 minutes. Allow to cool a little, then peel the slices off the parchment, put them in a bowl and cover with the olive oil. Leave to soak for a few hours if you can: the oil slightly softens the rind and, in turn, the slices flavour the oil.

When you're ready to cook, preheat the oven to 220°C fan (450°F), Gas Mark 8. Put a heavy roasting tin over a high heat and add 2 tablespoons of the olive oil. Season the fish and brown it all over – it will take about 5 minutes – then put it into the oven. Roast for 25 minutes; the flesh near the bone should be white, not glassy.

Make the salsa verde by putting all the ingredients, except the oil and lemon slices, in a food processor. Pulse-mix, pouring in the lemon-flavoured olive oil as you do so (but not the lemon slices yet). Scrape into a bowl. Chop the roast lemon slices and add them to the mixture, seasoning with a little pepper.

Heat the remaining 3 tablespoons of olive oil in a frying pan and sauté the garlic and rosemary until the garlic is golden. Serve the fish, either in the dish in which it has cooked or on a warmed platter, with the garlic and rosemary oil spooned over the top and the roast lemon salsa verde on the side.

MELISSA'S BUTTERFLIED LEG OF LAMB WITH YOGURT & HERB SAUCE

SERVES 8

FOR THE LAMB

1½ tablespoons cumin seeds

2 teaspoons coriander seeds

1 onion, chopped

finely grated zest and juice of 1 lime, plus lime wedges to serve

200g (7oz) natural yogurt

leaves from 8 mint sprigs, plus mint leaves to serve

25g (scant 1oz) coriander, plus coriander leaves to serve

6 garlic cloves, chopped

1 red chilli, deseeded if you want, chopped

2.5cm (1in) fresh root ginger, peeled and chopped

½ teaspoon sea salt flakes

½ teaspoon freshly ground black pepper

2.25kg (5lb) leg of lamb (pre-boned weight), boned and butterflied by your butcher

FOR THE SAUCE

250g (9oz) Greek yogurt

leaves from 8 mint sprigs

30g (1oz) coriander leaves

75ml (2½fl oz) extra virgin olive oil

2 garlic cloves, chopped

1 spring onion, trimmed and chopped

finely grated zest of 1 lime

2 tablespoons lime juice

45g (1¾oz) mayonnaise

sea salt flakes and freshly ground black pepper

This dish is from my friend (and fellow food writer) Melissa Clark. Melissa is the sort of cook who can have twenty people standing around in her kitchen while she throws dinner together. She's not remotely bothered about serving dishes she's never tried before and is a genuinely laidback cook. It's a joy to watch her (I'm going to cook like her when I grow up).

Toast the cumin and coriander seeds in a dry frying pan over a medium heat for about 2 minutes. Let them cool, then put them in a food processor with the onion, lime zest and juice, yogurt, mint and coriander, garlic, chilli and ginger, salt and pepper. Whizz until you have a paste.

Put the lamb in a dish, or a large plastic food bag, with the marinade, making sure the marinade goes into the flesh as well as the fatty side. Cover, or seal the bag, then chill for about 6 hours. Bring the meat to room temperature.

Preheat the oven to 210°C fan (425°F), Gas Mark 7.

Lift the lamb out of the marinade, shaking it off. Spread the meat out in a roasting tin, fatty side up, then roast for 15 minutes.

Reduce the oven temperature to 180°C fan (375°F), Gas Mark 5 and cook for another 15 minutes. The lamb will be pink. (If you want it more well done, increase the cooking time by 5 minutes.)

Remove from the oven, cover with foil, insulate with tea towels or old towels and leave to rest for 15 minutes.

To make the sauce, just put all the ingredients into the cleaned food processor bowl and blend. Taste for seasoning.

Slice the meat and arrange it on a warmed platter, spooning over any juices that have come out of it, and scatter with mint and coriander leaves and some sea salt flakes. Serve immediately, with lime wedges and the yogurt sauce.

BAKED SEA BASS WITH ASIAN DRESSING

This is a gorgeous looking dish and seems much more impressive than it really is (which is, after all, just roast fish). Serve with boiled rice and a salad, or with stir-fried pak choi.

Preheat the oven to 190°C fan (400°F), Gas Mark 6.

Put a double layer of baking parchment into a roasting tin or on to a roasting tray with a lip (or you can use one of the metal shelves in your oven, as long as it has a lip). It obviously needs to be big enough to hold the fish.

Put the chilli, ginger, garlic, the 10g (¼oz) of coriander and the lime zest into a mortar with some salt and pound them together, adding 1 tablespoon of the oil, until you have a rough paste. Add the lime juice.

Put the fish on the baking parchment. Make 4 slits in each side of the fish, without cutting through the bone, and push the paste into these. Put the spring onions into the belly of the fish. Rub the rest of the oil over the fish on both sides and season with salt. Bake for 30 minutes, then check for doneness: the flesh near the bone at the thickest part should be white, not glassy.

Make the dressing by mixing together the lime juice, sugar, fish sauce and chilli. Serve the fish with the dressing on the side, or spoon it over the top. Scatter with the 5g (⅛oz) coriander leaves and serve with lime wedges.

SERVES 6

FOR THE FISH

1 red chilli, halved, deseeded and chopped

3cm (1¼in) fresh root ginger, peeled and finely grated

3 garlic cloves, finely grated

10g (¼oz) coriander leaves, roughly chopped, plus 5g (⅛oz) coriander leaves to serve

finely grated zest of 2 limes, plus the juice of ½ lime, plus lime wedges to serve

sea salt flakes

2 tablespoons groundnut oil

1.8kg (4lb) sea bass, gutted, scaled and washed

6 spring onions, trimmed and roughly chopped

FOR THE DRESSING

juice of 1 lime

2 tablespoons caster sugar

6 tablespoons fish sauce

1 red chilli, halved, deseeded and very finely sliced

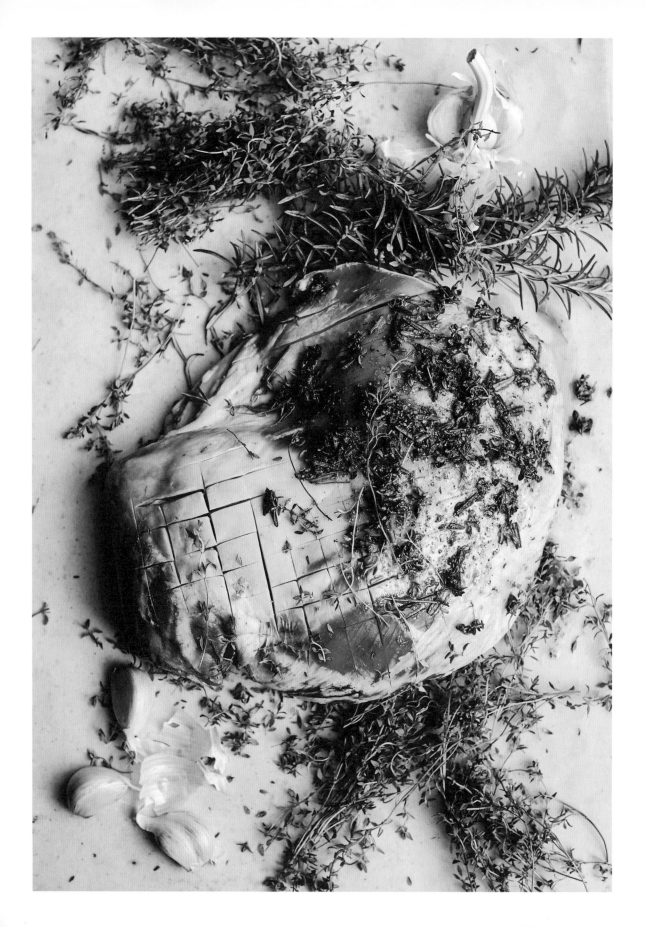

LAMB SHOULDER WITH HONEY, HERBS & LEMON-CAPER RELISH

This really shows what roasting can do. You put a big square of meat – not a prime cut – into the oven and, with a little attention (just make sure there's always some liquid in the roasting tin) and a lot of herbs you end up with a melting mass of sweet meat.

Preheat the oven to 200°C fan (410°F), Gas Mark 6½. Put all the herb leaves (not the whole sprigs) and the dried oregano in a mortar with the salt, pepper and olive oil and grind everything together. Score the fat of the lamb – without cutting into the meat – and rub the herb mixture all over it, pushing it down into the slashes. Scatter the rest of the herb sprigs and all the garlic cloves in a roasting tin that will hold the lamb snugly. Set the lamb on top; the garlic and the herbs must be underneath, or they will burn. Squeeze the lemon juice over, then pour half the wine into the tin. Cover with a double layer of foil, sealing it tightly round the edges.

Put the tin into the oven and immediately reduce the temperature to 140°C fan (300°F), Gas Mark 2 and cook for 3½–4 hours. Check every so often to see whether you need to add any more wine (just enough to keep the pan moist). The meat is ready when it is falling off the bone. When there are just 30 minutes cooking time left, drizzle the honey on top. Once it's cooked, lay some towels over the foil and leave the lamb to rest for 15 minutes.

To make the relish, remove the lemon zest from 1 lemon with a zester, then roughly chop it. Peel the white pith away from that lemon, then remove all the peel and pith from the other. Remove the flesh from both: using a very sharp knife, cut between each segment and carefully ease it out. Chop the flesh into little pieces and put it in a bowl with the zest, olive oil, honey, vinegar and lemon juice. Chop the capers and add them to the bowl with the garlic. Stir and taste for balance: remember this will be served with fatty lamb that can take a relish that's assertive and quite acidic. When you are about to serve, add the mint leaves (they turn black if they sit in acid for too long).

SERVES 6

FOR THE LAMB

leaves from ½ bunch of lemon thyme, plus another dozen whole sprigs

6 rosemary sprigs, leaves removed and chopped, plus another dozen whole sprigs

1 tablespoon dried oregano

1 tablespoon sea salt flakes

freshly ground black pepper

2 tablespoons extra virgin olive oil

2kg (4lb 8oz) shoulder of lamb on the bone

1 head of garlic, cloves separated

juice of 1 lemon

250ml (9fl oz) dry white wine

2 tablespoons honey (a floral or herbal type, such as lavender or thyme)

FOR THE RELISH

2 unwaxed lemons

4 tablespoons extra virgin olive oil

2 tablespoons honey

1 tablespoon white balsamic vinegar

2 tablespoons lemon juice, or to taste

2 tablespoons capers, drained, rinsed and patted dry

½ small garlic clove, finely grated

leaves from 12 mint sprigs, torn

GARLIC & OREGANO CHICKEN WITH CHIPOTLE ALLIOLI

SERVES 6

FOR THE CHICKEN

1.8kg (4lb) chicken

10 garlic cloves, finely grated

½ tablespoon sea salt flakes

1 red chilli, halved, deseeded and finely chopped

1½ tablespoons dried oregano

2 tablespoons extra virgin olive oil

juice of 1 lemon

roast sweet potato wedges, to serve (optional)

FOR THE CHIPOTLE ALLIOLI

1 egg yolk

1 teaspoon Dijon mustard

2 garlic cloves, finely grated

115ml (3¾fl oz) mixed groundnut and extra virgin olive oils

1 tablespoon chipotle paste

lemon juice, to taste

sea salt flakes and freshly ground black pepper

If you can buy dried Mexican oregano, which is a little different from the European type, then do (you can find it online). The allioli may seem an effort too far, if so, mix some good bought mayonnaise with chipotle paste.

To spatchcock the chicken, set the bird on a work surface, breast side down, legs towards you. Using good kitchen scissors, or poultry shears, cut through the flesh and bone along both sides of the backbone. Remove the backbone (you can keep it for stock). Open the chicken, turn it over, then flatten it by pressing hard on the breastbone with the heel of your hand. You'll feel it breaking and flattening under your hand. Remove any big globules of fat and neaten the ragged bits of skin. Now you have a spatchcocked bird.

Put the chicken into a dish that fits in your fridge. Mix all the other ingredients to make a marinade. Gently loosen the skin of the breast, pushing your fingers between the skin and flesh. Work your way under the skin down to the legs. Spoon some marinade in here, then spread it over the chicken on both sides. Cover and put into the fridge for a few hours if you can, turning it once. Bring the bird to room temperature.

Preheat the oven to 190°C fan (400°F), Gas Mark 6. Put the chicken into a roasting tin and roast for 1 hour, basting a few times during the cooking.

Make the allioli while the chicken is cooking. Mix the egg yolk, mustard and garlic in a bowl. Using electric beaters or a wooden spoon, gradually add the oils in little drops, making sure each is incorporated before you add the next. If it splits, start again with a new egg yolk and gradually add the curdled mixture. Add the chipotle paste, lemon juice to taste (start with about 1 tablespoon) and seasoning. If you're making this more than 1 hour ahead, cover and keep it in the fridge, stirring it when you take it out. (Don't serve it cold from the fridge.)

Check the chicken is cooked properly (*see* page 185). Cut into pieces and serve with the chipotle allioli. Roast sweet potato wedges are brilliant with it.

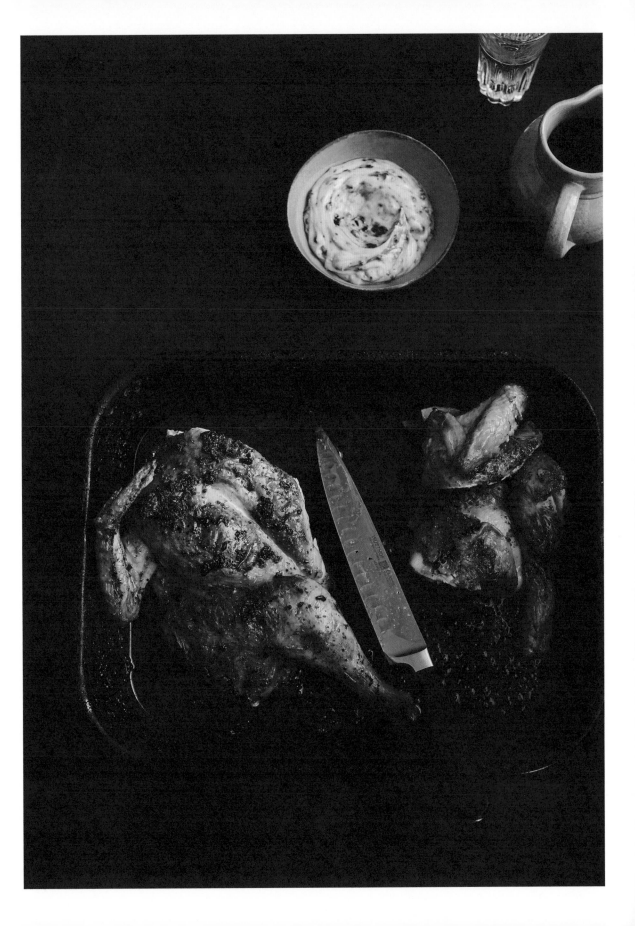

ROAST LAMB WITH APPLES, SOMERSET CIDER BRANDY & CREAM

Very old-fashioned (it's the cream), but very good. A dish to have with cider. I make it with English cider brandy but, of course, you can use French Calvados.

Preheat the oven to 200°C fan (410°F), Gas Mark 6½.

Make small incisions all over the lamb with a very sharp knife, then stuff each slit with a sliver of garlic and a little bit of thyme. Rub the butter all over the lamb, stuffing some of it down inside the incisions. Put into a roasting tin big enough to hold the lamb and – eventually – the apples, too. Season.

Roast for 20 minutes, then reduce the oven temperature to 180°C fan (375°F), Gas Mark 5. Pour 200ml (7fl oz) of the cider around the joint, then put the apples in, too. Roast for 45 minutes. This will give you very pink lamb. If you prefer it more well done, then cook for a little longer.

Pour the cooking juices into a jug, but be careful with the apples as you do so, because you want them to stay intact. Leave the lamb and the apples to sit and rest, covered and insulated with towels, while you make the sauce.

Add ice cubes to the cooking juices to drive the fat to the surface; skim it off.

Put the cider brandy, cooking juices and the remaining cider into a saucepan and bring to the boil. Boil until the liquid is reduced by two-thirds, then add the stock. Boil until this, too, is reduced by two-thirds, then add the cream. Boil until slightly syrupy (it doesn't have to be thick, just not as thin as the cooking juices were). If you want the sauce to be a little sweeter, add the apple jelly and allow it to melt in the sauce. Serve the lamb on a warmed platter with the apples around it and the cider sauce in a jug.

SERVES 6

1.5kg (3lb 5oz) leg of lamb

6 garlic cloves, cut into fine slivers

leaves from 4 thyme sprigs

25g (scant 1oz) unsalted butter

sea salt flakes and freshly ground black pepper

500ml (18fl oz) dry cider

6 small tart eating apples

4 tablespoons Somerset cider brandy, or Calvados

500ml (18fl oz) lamb stock

125ml (4fl oz) double cream

2 teaspoons apple jelly (optional)

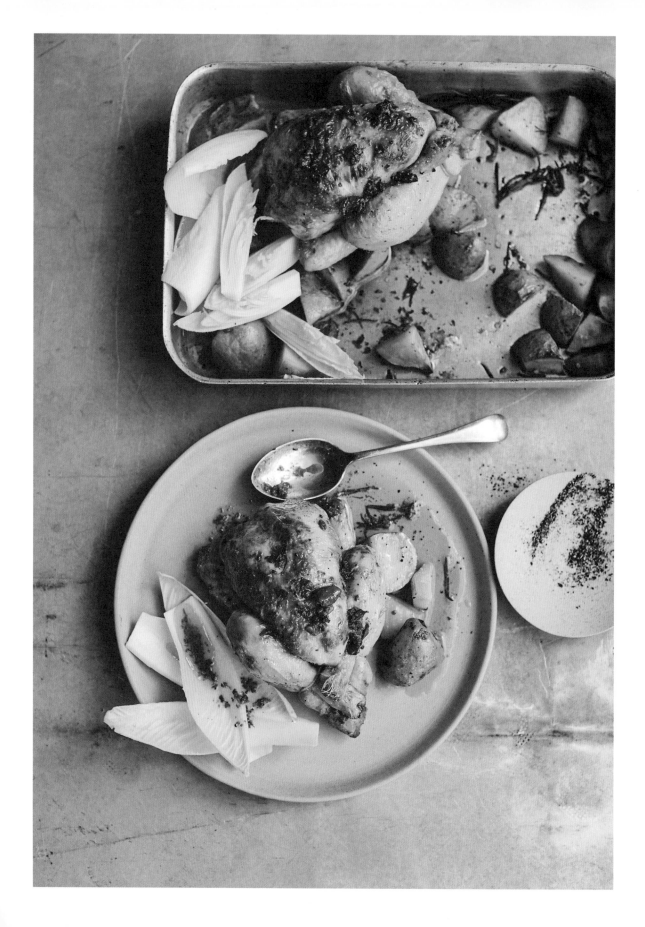

POUSSINS WITH BLACK OLIVE & ANCHOVY BUTTER

SERVES 4

35g (1¼oz) pitted black olives (pitted weight), finely chopped

35g (1¼oz) anchovies, drained of oil and chopped

75g (2¾oz) unsalted butter, softened

1 garlic clove, finely grated

sea salt flakes and freshly ground black pepper

450g (1lb) waxy potatoes, such as Charlotte, scrubbed

½–1 teaspoon chilli flakes

leaves from 4 rosemary sprigs

2 tablespoons extra virgin olive oil

4 poussins

green salad, or roasted vegetables, to serve

Ever since I read about Alice Waters serving black olive and anchovy butter at Chez Panisse, I have been making black olive and anchovy butter. This couldn't be simpler, but the end result delivers much more than you expect… though, on reflection, you can't go wrong with chicken and melting butter, salty with anchovies and inky with olives. Serve with watercress or roast red peppers and baby potatoes cooked with rosemary (see page 107).

Preheat the oven to 180°C fan (375°F), Gas Mark 5.

Put the olives, anchovies, butter, garlic and black pepper into a mortar and pestle and either pound or mash. (You can also do this with a fork and bowl, though the ingredients don't end up as well incorporated.)

Cut the potatoes into chunks – roughly 2cm (¾in) square – and put them into a roasting tin in which they can lie in a single layer, with room for the poussins on top. Add the chilli flakes, rosemary leaves, seasoning and about two-thirds of the olive oil and toss all this with the potatoes.

Gently lift the skin on the breast of the poussins – be careful not to tear it – and push the butter down under the skin of each bird (if you can get as far as the legs, pushing some in there too, so much the better, but it's hard to do this without ripping the skin). Don't use all the butter, keep some for melting on the poussins once they're cooked.

Put the poussins on top of the potatoes, brush the remaining oil on the birds and season. Roast for 50 minutes. Transfer the poussins and the potatoes to a warmed platter and put some of the remaining butter to melt on top of the poussins. Serve immediately.

This is lovely with a green salad, but some kind of roasted vegetable is good too (aubergines, fennel, tomatoes or peppers, depending on the time of year).

BAKED ANCHOVY-STUFFED RED MULLET WITH FENNEL

They are such wonderful little fish, red mullet, both because of their colour and small tender flakes, and because they arrive in winter looking as if they've come straight from a blue-sky summer. There's quite a lot of stuffing here – more than will, strictly, fit inside the fish – but let it spill out into the dish. The fish aren't in the oven for long, so the stuffing doesn't get dry, it just soaks up the juices.

Preheat the oven to 180°C fan (375°F), Gas Mark 5.

Remove any fronds from the fennel and reserve. Trim the tips – they are coarse – quarter the bulb(s) and trim the base of each piece. Slice the fennel lengthways into slim wedges, about 5mm (¼in) at the thickest part. Toss the fennel into a roasting tin or a 30cm (12in) shallow casserole with the onion, salt and pepper, a couple of tablespoons of olive oil and the lemon juice. Bake in the oven for 15 minutes.

Mix all the ingredients for the stuffing with some seasoning and add a little olive oil (the mixture should be moist, but not sloppy). Season the cavities of the fish, then stuff them with the anchovy mixture, pushing it up into the head so you can get plenty inside each one.

Put the fish on top of the vegetables, season, then drizzle with a little olive oil. Scatter on the fennel fronds.

Bake for 20 minutes. The flesh should be opaque near the bone at the thickest part – not at all glassy – and the vegetables tender. Serve with lemon wedges and good bread.

SERVES 4

FOR THE FISH AND FENNEL

1 large or 2 medium fennel bulbs

1 red onion, sliced into fine wedges no more than 4mm (¼in) at the thick end

sea salt flakes and freshly ground black pepper

extra virgin olive oil

juice of 1 lemon, plus lemon wedges to serve

4 medium whole red mullet, about 350g (12oz) each, gutted, scaled and washed

good bread, to serve

FOR THE STUFFING

50g (1¾oz) anchovies, drained of oil and finely chopped

50g (1¾oz) fresh white breadcrumbs

2 garlic cloves, finely grated

1 plum tomato, finely chopped

1 tablespoon finely chopped flat leaf parsley leaves

ENDLESS EMBELLISHMENTS

Roasted foods – whole chickens or legs of lamb, fish, root vegetables or softer Mediterranean vegetables – are basic; it isn't difficult to cook them. But their character can be completely changed depending on what you serve with them. These salsas and relishes – accessories, if you like – bring their own personality and can be made while your chicken thighs or peppers are being transformed by the heat of the oven. Most of them require only chopping and mixing. Each serves 4–6.

ANCHOVY, OLIVE & CAPER DRESSING

Gently heat 200ml (7fl oz) of extra virgin olive oil and add 2 finely sliced garlic cloves. Cook for 1 minute, then add 12 drained, chopped anchovies. Cook gently, pressing with the back of a spoon until they 'melt'. Add about a dozen chopped pitted black olives, a good pinch of chilli flakes, 1½ tablespoons of soaked, drained and patted dry capers, 1½ tablespoons of lemon juice and 2 tablespoons of finely chopped flat leaf parsley leaves. Good with steak or roast fillet of beef or lamb, roast tomatoes or peppers, or roast fish.

ARTICHOKE & BASIL MAYO

This is based on a recipe from the American chef and vegetable maestro Joshua McFadden. It's wonderful with roasted Mediterranean vegetables, especially tomatoes, slices of aubergine and peppers; try it with those in ciabatta sandwiches. It's also lovely with roast chicken and lamb: have it on the side with basic chicken thighs roasted with potatoes and onions, or lamb loin (*see* page 22), or roast sea bass or bream. Put 6 drained jarred artichoke hearts into a blender with a generous handful of basil leaves and pulse a few times. Add 200g (7oz) of mayonnaise and 1 egg yolk. Whizz, then add 1 tablespoon of lemon juice. With the motor running, gradually add 4 tablespoons of extra virgin olive oil. Taste for seasoning and balance: you might want a little more lemon juice.

YOGURT & PRESERVED LEMON DRESSING

Chop the flesh and rind of 2 preserved lemons – discard any seeds – and stir it into 160g (5¾oz) of Greek yogurt along with 2 tablespoons of brine from the preserved lemon jar and 1 garlic clove, finely grated. Serve with roast tomatoes, aubergines, peppers or pumpkin.

ARTICHOKE & GREEN OLIVE TAPENADE

Purée 150g (5½oz) of drained jarred artichoke hearts, 35g (1¼oz) of pitted green olives, 30g (1oz) of blanched almonds, 1 garlic clove, chopped, a pinch of chilli flakes, the juice of ½ lemon and 5 tablespoons of extra virgin olive oil with salt and pepper. Particularly good with fish, chicken, roast tomatoes and peppers.

AVOCADO, CORIANDER & PICKLED CHILLI RELISH

Chop the flesh of 2 just-ripe avocados and put it in a bowl with the juice of 1 lime, 200g (7oz) of well-flavoured tomatoes, finely chopped, 2 spring onions, also finely chopped, 1 teaspoon of ground cumin, 1 red chilli, deseeded and finely chopped, 3 tablespoons of finely chopped coriander leaves, 2 pickled chillies, chopped, 1 garlic clove, finely grated, 5 tablespoons of extra virgin olive oil, salt and pepper. Taste: you may need more lime juice. Serve with baked potatoes (regular or sweet) along with soured cream, baked fish of any type, or roast chicken or pork.

GEORGIAN ADJIKA

Put 4 garlic cloves and 1 celery stick, both roughly chopped, into a food processor with 4 red chillies and 1 red pepper, both chopped and deseeded. Pulse-blend to a salsa-like mixture. Add 25g (scant 1oz) each of dill and coriander leaves and pulse-blend again. Scrape into a bowl and add seasoning, 3½ tablespoons of red wine vinegar and 4 tablespoons of extra virgin olive oil. Good with chicken and lamb. It is hot, so be careful. I serve it with yogurt (in case you need to put the fire out).

THAI NAM JIM DRESSING
Put 2 garlic cloves, chopped, into a mortar with a pinch of sea salt flakes – the salt acts as an abrasive – and the leaves from a 35g (1¼oz) bunch of coriander, any coarse stalks discarded, roughly chopped, and pound to a rough paste. Add 1 red chilli, chopped (leave the seeds in) and 2 tablespoons of palm sugar or soft light brown sugar and pound some more. Stir in 2 tablespoons of fish sauce, 2½ tablespoons of lime juice and 2 small shallots, very finely chopped. Good with baked fish and roast chicken or pork.

ROAST PEPPER, CAPER & PRESERVED LEMON RELISH
In a bowl, stir together ½ roasted pepper, flesh chopped, 2 tablespoons of white balsamic vinegar, 6 tablespoons of extra virgin olive oil, the rind of 1 preserved lemon, finely chopped, 1 tablespoon of rinsed, drained and patted dry capers, 1 red chilli, deseeded and finely chopped and 3 tablespoons of chopped coriander leaves (mint is good as well). Lovely with roast fish or lamb: try it with lamb loin fillets (*see* page 22), cooked without the peas.

SMOKY CHIMICHURRI
A riff on a classic sauce used in Argentina and Uruguay and perfect with beef, though it's also good on potatoes and roast tomatoes. Put 4 garlic cloves, chopped, into a food processor with 50g (1¾oz) of flat leaf parsley leaves and 65g (2¼oz) of coriander leaves and add 5 tablespoons of extra virgin olive oil (a buttery one). Pour in 75ml (2½fl oz) of cider vinegar and ¾ teaspoon of smoked paprika. Pulse-blend, then stir in 1 green chilli, deseeded and finely chopped, 4 trimmed and chopped spring onions and salt and pepper.

HOT SOUR-SWEET ASIAN SAUCE
This – which is quite like Vietnamese *nuoc cham*, but not the same – is intensely salty, sour and sweet and can sit in the fridge for about 5 days. It's worth making in quantity, though you can also halve it. Mix 75ml (2½fl oz) of boiling water (less if you want the sauce to be more intense) with 4 tablespoons of caster sugar or palm sugar. Stir well to dissolve the sugar. Add 6–8 red chillies, halved, deseeded and chopped, 125ml (4fl oz) of fish sauce, 75ml (2½fl oz) of rice vinegar, the juice of 1–2 limes, 4 garlic cloves, finely grated and 2cm (¾in) of fresh root ginger, peeled and finely grated. Great with roast chicken and fish, though I find it totally addictive and would put it on nearly anything.

MANGO & TAMARIND RELISH
Peel 2 under-ripe mangoes and remove the flesh as neatly as possible. Cut it into small cubes and put in a saucepan with 1 red and 1 green chilli, both halved, deseeded and finely chopped. Add 2 tablespoons of tamarind paste, 1 tablespoon of soft light brown sugar and 50ml (2fl oz) of water. Set over a medium heat and cook for 4 minutes, stirring from time to time (you can serve this raw, but I like it a little cooked). Remove from the heat and add the juice of 1 lime. Just before serving, stir in 2 tablespoons of chopped coriander leaves. Good with roast chicken, pork or baked fish, such as mackerel, bream or sea bass. This takes on an Indian accent if you add a little ground cumin, turmeric and ginger.

PARSLEY, TOMATO & POMEGRANATE RELISH
Halve and deseed 135g (4¾oz) of tomatoes and finely chop the flesh. Mix in the finely chopped leaves from 115g (4oz) of flat leaf parsley, ½ small red onion, finely chopped, 1 small garlic clove, finely grated, 1 tablespoon of lemon juice, 4 tablespoons of extra virgin olive oil, 1 tablespoon of pomegranate molasses, the seeds from ½ pomegranate and seasoning. Serve with fish, chicken, lamb, or roast Mediterranean vegetables.

POT-ROAST INDIAN-SPICED CHICKEN WITH COCONUT

This dish is not from India. I just made it up to feed my longing for Indian spices. It's slightly sweet – because of the sweet potatoes – and rich with ginger and coconut.

Preheat the oven to 200°C fan (410°F), Gas Mark 6½.

Start by making the spice paste. Put the mustard seeds in a frying pan over a medium heat and cook until the seeds start to pop (this happens in less than a minute). Add the peppercorns, cumin and coriander seeds, garam masala, turmeric and cinnamon. Cook for 2 minutes.

Scrape the spice mix into a mini food processor with the chillies, garlic, ginger, malt vinegar and oil. Process to a paste. If you don't have a mini food processor, put the dry spices into a mortar, add the chillies, garlic and ginger and grind to a paste, gradually adding the vinegar and oil. Rub about half the spice paste all over the chicken and season the bird in the cavity and outside.

Heat the oil in a casserole big enough to take the chicken. Sauté the onion until soft and golden, then add the garlic, ginger and the rest of the spice paste and cook for 2 minutes. Add the tomatoes, seasoning and sugar, if using, and cook for another 4 minutes or so, or until it has reduced a little and isn't quite as sloppy. Add the coconut cream and bring to just under the boil, then put the chicken in with the sweet potatoes, spoon over the juices and put into the oven, uncovered.

Cook for 20 minutes, then cover, reduce the oven temperature to 180°C fan (375°F), Gas Mark 5 and cook for a further 30 minutes. Spoon the juices over the bird and return it to the oven for a final 15 minutes, uncovered. Check for doneness by piercing the chicken between the leg and the main body: the juices that run out should be clear, with no trace of pink.

Scatter the coriander over everything and serve the chicken from the pot. You'll need boiled rice or naan bread on the side, and maybe some raita.

SERVES 6

FOR THE SPICE PASTE

1 teaspoon black mustard seeds

1 teaspoon black peppercorns

1 tablespoon cumin seeds

1 tablespoon coriander seeds

1 teaspoon garam masala

½ teaspoon ground turmeric

¼ teaspoon ground cinnamon

2 red chillies, halved and deseeded

3 garlic cloves, finely grated

2cm (¾in) fresh root ginger, peeled and chopped

2 tablespoons malt vinegar

1 tablespoon groundnut oil

FOR THE CHICKEN

1.8kg (4lb) chicken

sea salt flakes and freshly ground black pepper

1 tablespoon groundnut oil

1 large onion, finely chopped

3 garlic cloves, finely grated

2cm (¾in) fresh root ginger, peeled and finely grated

400g can of cherry tomatoes in thick juice

1 teaspoon soft light brown sugar (optional)

400g can of coconut cream

400g (14oz) sweet potatoes, scrubbed, cut into chunks (peel them if you want to)

leaves from a 30g (1oz) bunch of coriander, roughly chopped

boiled rice, naan bread and raita (optional), to serve

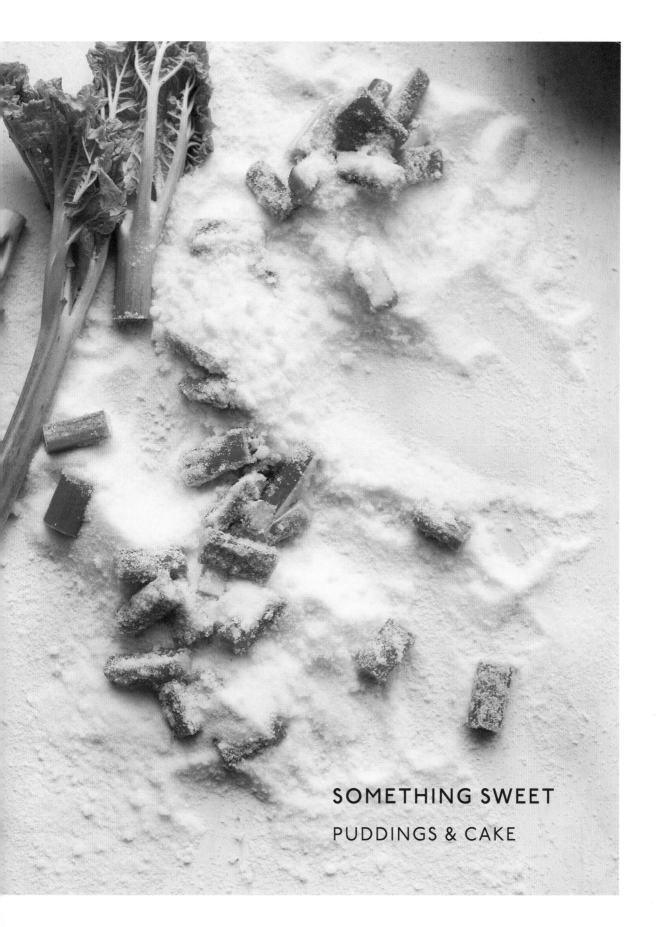

SOMETHING SWEET

PUDDINGS & CAKE

CHOCOLATE & RED WINE CAKE

OK, not exactly bung-it-in-the-oven, but nevertheless an easy cake that can be served for tea as well as for pudding. The orange-red wine balance is delicate, so don't add any more zest than suggested otherwise the flavour of the wine will disappear. Astonishingly, despite all that chocolate, you can taste it.

Preheat the oven to 170°C fan (350°F), Gas Mark 4. Butter a 23cm (9in) springform cake tin and line the base with baking parchment.

Put the chocolate in a heatproof bowl set over a pan of gently simmering water (the base of the bowl shouldn't touch the water). Melt the chocolate, stirring a little to help it along. Remove the bowl and leave it to cool a little.

Cream the butter and sugar with electric beaters until lighter in colour and fluffy. Gradually add the eggs, beating well after each addition.

In a bowl, sift together the cocoa, flour, baking powder and salt, then fold this into the batter. Stir in the red wine and the orange zest, then the melted chocolate. Scrape into the prepared tin and bake for 40 minutes, or until a skewer inserted into the middle comes out clean. Allow the cake to cool in the tin, then turn it out on to a wire rack to cool completely.

For the glaze, put the chocolate into a heatproof bowl and melt as before. Stir in the cream with the port until the mixture is smooth, then whisk in the icing sugar. Leave this to cool a little (though don't leave it until it has set), then pour it over the cake. Let the glaze set a bit before serving.

A glass of red dessert wine (look for Maury from France, or the Greek sweet red wine, Mavrodaphne) is lovely with this.

FOR THE CAKE

200g (7oz) unsalted butter, at room temperature, plus more for the tin

150g (5½oz) 70% cocoa solids dark chocolate, broken into pieces

250g (9oz) soft dark brown sugar

4 large eggs, at room temperature, lightly beaten

25g (scant 1oz) cocoa powder

250g (9oz) plain flour

1 teaspoon baking powder

pinch of fine sea salt

100ml (3½fl oz) red wine; a merlot or cabernet is perfect

finely grated zest of 1 orange

FOR THE GLAZE

130g (4½oz) 70% cocoa solids dark chocolate, broken into pieces

115g (4oz) double cream

2 tablespoons port

3 tablespoons icing sugar, sifted

BAKED RICE PUDDING WITH
QUINCE JELLY & BLACKBERRIES

It took me years to get baked rice pudding right (I kept trying to cook it too quickly). The nutmeggy skin and swollen creamy grains are the gorgeous result of slow baking in the oven. If you have sweet apple jelly, or other sweet home-made jellies, use those instead of quince jelly.

Preheat the oven to 150°C fan (325°F), Gas Mark 3 and butter a 2-litre (3½-pint) baking dish.

Put the butter, sugar, pudding rice, milk and cream into a saucepan and bring gently to the boil, stirring to help the sugar dissolve. Add the salt, nutmeg, lemon zest and vanilla extract and return to a simmer.

Simmer for about 4 minutes, stirring all the time, until you can feel that the rice grains have become slightly (only slightly) swollen. Pour the mixture into the prepared dish and bake for 2 hours. By this time the rice should be creamy and cooked, but shouldn't be dry or overly sticky.

As the pudding looks beautiful baked – it develops a lovely golden skin on top – take it to the table in the pudding dish and put the quince jelly and the blackberries in separate serving bowls, so people can help themselves.

SERVES 4–6

FOR THE RICE PUDDING

50g (1¾oz) unsalted butter, plus more for the dish

35g (1¼oz) caster sugar

100g (3½oz) short-grain pudding rice

1 litre (1¾ pints) whole milk

150ml (5fl oz) double cream

pinch of salt

lots of freshly grated nutmeg

finely grated zest of ½ unwaxed lemon

¼ teaspoon vanilla extract

TO SERVE

quince jelly

150g (5½oz) blackberries

SERVES 6

FOR THE CREAM

200ml (7fl oz) double cream

150g (5½oz) Greek yogurt

3–4 heaped tablespoons
muscovado sugar

FOR THE PLUMS

800g (1lb 12oz) plums
(preferably crimson-fleshed),
halved and pitted

2 globes of stem ginger,
very finely chopped

75g (2¾oz) soft light
brown sugar

½ teaspoon ground ginger

3 broad strips of lime zest,
plus juice of 1 lime

150ml (5fl oz) dark rum, plus
3 tablespoons

GINGER-ROAST PLUMS WITH LIME, RUM & MUSCOVADO CREAM

This is best made with plums that have a strong flavour and will hold their shape: crimson tart-sweet fruits, rather than soft English Victorias. You need to judge for doneness, as the cooking time depends on how ripe your plums are (they can take as long as 30 minutes if they're hard), but roasting does transform the most unpromising and under-ripe specimens. You can also make this dish with apricots, but they take a bit less cooking time.

Make the cream about 12 hours before you want to serve it. Lightly whip the double cream, then fold in the yogurt. Put this in a bowl and sprinkle evenly with the sugar. Cover with cling film and put in the fridge. The sugar will become soft and treacly.

Preheat the oven to 180°C fan (375°F), Gas Mark 5.

Put the plums into a roasting tin or a big ovenproof dish or gratin dish in which they can lie in a single layer (snugly; you don't want the juices around them to reduce and burn). Arrange the fruits so they are cut sides up. Scatter the stem ginger around the plums. Mix the sugar with the ground ginger and sprinkle it over the top. Squeeze the lime juice over and tuck the pieces of lime zest under the fruits, then pour the 150ml (5fl oz) rum around them.

Bake for 15–30 minutes (how long it takes depends on the ripeness of the plums). The fruit should be tender when pierced with a sharp knife, but not collapsing. Leave to cool completely; the juices should thicken as they cool. If they aren't thick enough, drain off the juices and boil them in a saucepan until they become more syrupy. Add the remaining 3 tablespooons of rum. Serve the plums, at room temperature, with the muscovado cream.

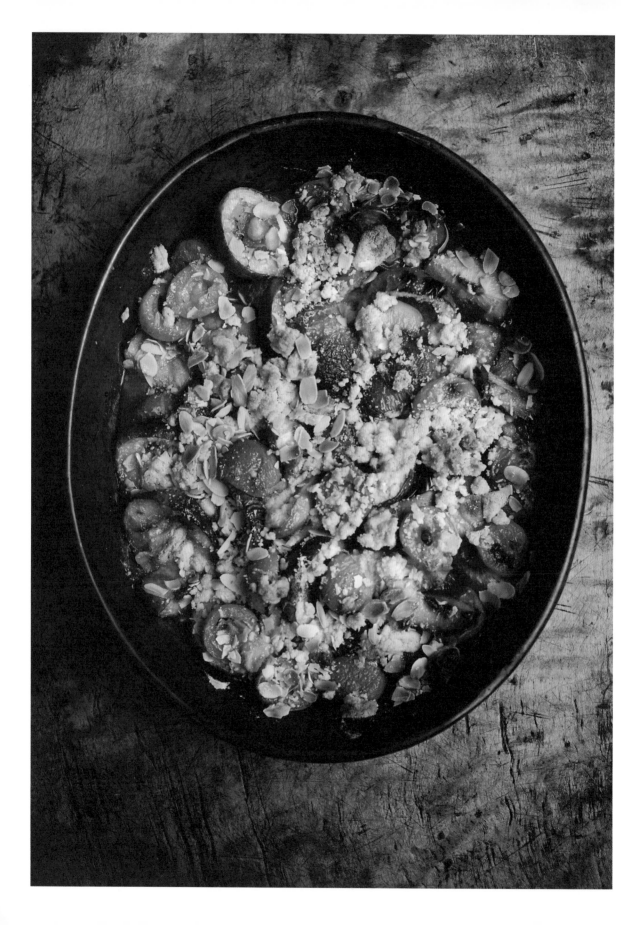

ROAST STONE FRUIT WITH ALMOND & ORANGE FLOWER CRUMBS

I like crumble – who doesn't? – but it can be a bit stodgy, more about the crumble than the fruit. In this dish, the fruit shines more – it gets gorgeous caramelized edges – and the 'crumble' is rich with nuggets of marzipan and scented with flower water. This is a big pudding and I usually have leftovers, but that means I can eat them for breakfast.

Preheat the oven to 200°C fan (410°F), Gas Mark 6½.

Halve and pit all the fruit. Cut the larger fruits – peaches and nectarines – into 6 wedges (each half into 3). Put all the fruit into a dish, sprinkle it with the sugar, lemon zest and juice and turn it over with your hands. Take 30g (1oz) of the marzipan and put little nuggets of this in among the fruit. Break the rest of the marzipan into little balls, but reserve it for now. Sprinkle the flower water over the fruit.

Put the flour, ground almonds and butter into a bowl and rub them together with your fingertips. You want to end up with a mixture that looks like small pebbles and gravel. Sprinkle this over the top of the fruit, then put the balls of marzipan on top, too, leaving patches of the fruit completely uncovered. Bake for 30 minutes, or until the fruit is completely tender and the crumbs are golden, scattering over the flaked almonds halfway through the cooking time.

Leave to cool a bit (I like it at room temperature, but you might prefer it warm) and dust a little icing sugar over the top, if you want.

Serve with whipped cream or crème fraîche.

SERVES 8

900g (2lb) stone fruit: a mixture of peaches, nectarines, plums and apricots is good here

2 tablespoons caster sugar

finely grated zest of 1 unwaxed lemon, plus juice of ½ lemon

65g (2½oz) good-quality marzipan

½ tablespoon orange flower water

50g (1¾oz) plain flour

30g (1oz) ground almonds

65g (2½oz) cold unsalted butter, cut into cubes

15g (½oz) flaked almonds

icing sugar, to dust (optional)

whipped cream or crème fraîche, to serve

RHUBARB WITH DAMSON GIN, ORANGE & ROSEMARY

SERVES 4

700g (1lb 9oz) forced rhubarb stalks, all about the same thickness

125g (4½oz) granulated sugar

finely grated zest of ½ orange

7 tablespoons damson gin

3 tablespoons orange juice

2 rosemary sprigs, bruised

whipped cream or pouring cream, to serve

I usually bake rhubarb in the oven, rather than poaching it. This way, the pieces stay intact, though you still have to be sure that they don't overcook and collapse, so keep an eye on the dish. Cinnamon, ginger or star anise work well too, instead of rosemary.

Preheat the oven to 170°C fan (350°F), Gas Mark 4.

Remove any leaves from the rhubarb and trim the bases. Cut into 3cm (1¼in) lengths and put them into a large ovenproof dish. Scatter the sugar and zest on top and turn it all over with your hands, then pour in the damson gin, orange juice and 2 tablespoons water, and finally tuck the rosemary sprigs under the rhubarb.

Cover tightly with foil, then bake for 30 minutes or so (the time this takes will depend on the thickness of the stalks, start checking after 20 minutes by piercing them with a sharp knife). The rhubarb should be tender, but holding its shape and not collapsing.

Remove from the oven and leave to cool a bit in the dish. Eat warm, at room temperature or chilled, with whipped cream or pouring cream.

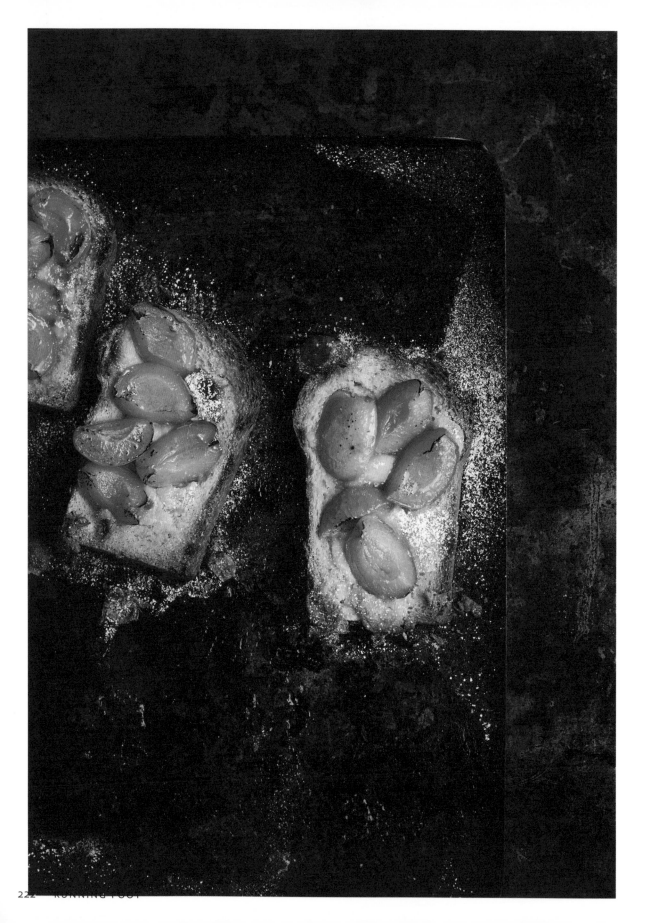

APRICOT & ALMOND CROÛTES

This is really a cheat's Bostock, the French creation where brioche is topped with jam and frangipane (and sometimes fruit) and baked. It is definitely more than just fruit on toast, but it's as simple as that. You need ripe apricots. Unripe fruits won't soften in the time they're in the oven, so, if you can't find good apricots, plums would be better and are just as lovely. And get good brioche; some supermarket brands are a bit dry.

SERVES 6

6 thick slices of brioche

30g (1oz) caster sugar, plus 4 teaspoons

50–75ml (2–2½fl oz) amaretto, or Marsala

75g (2¾oz) very soft unsalted butter

110g (3¾oz) good-quality marzipan, broken into small chunks

12 small ripe apricots, or 6 plums, pitted and quartered

juice of ½ lemon

35g (1¼oz) flaked almonds (optional)

icing sugar, to dust (optional)

crème fraîche or clotted cream, to serve

Preheat the oven to 190°C fan (400°F), Gas Mark 6.

Put the brioche slices on a baking sheet or in a roasting tin in which they can lie in a single layer.

Spoon the 30g (1oz) sugar into a small heatproof bowl and pour in 50ml (2fl oz) boiling water. Stir until dissolved, then leave this simple syrup to cool. Stir in the amaretto or Marsala.

Spoon the cooled syrup over the brioche slices, covering both sides.

Carefully, because the brioche will be very soft now, butter each slice on both sides.

Arrange chunks of marzipan on top, then add the apricot quarters. Squeeze on the lemon juice and sprinkle with the 4 teaspoons of caster sugar.

Bake for 25 minutes, sprinkling on the almonds, if using, after 15 minutes. The apricots should be tender and the bread and marzipan both golden.

Leave to cool a little (the slices will be very hot), then sift over some icing sugar, if you want. Serve with crème fraîche or clotted cream.

SOUR CHERRY, ROSE & CARDAMOM BRIOCHE PUDDING

SERVES 8

125g (4½oz) dried sour cherries

about 100ml (3½fl oz) unsweetened pomegranate juice

300ml (½ pint) double cream

300ml (½ pint) whole milk

pinch of sea salt

seeds from 2 cardamom pods, ground

3 large eggs, plus 1 large egg yolk

150g (5½oz) caster sugar

250g (9oz) brioche loaf

35g (1¼oz) unsalted butter, softened

1 teaspoon rose water, or to taste

squeeze of lemon or lime juice

icing sugar, to dust

I apologize. I nearly always include a recipe for bread pudding in my books, because I keep making new versions and am always in love with the latest incarnation. Get good fat dried sour cherries for this (and make it with fresh cherries when in season). The combination of cardamom and rose water is heaven, but don't overdo the spice. It should feel as if cardamom has 'walked through' a dish, leaving its perfume behind; it should never dominate.

Put the dried cherries in a small saucepan and add enough pomegranate juice to just cover. Bring to the boil, then take off the heat and leave the cherries to sit and plump up (they need at least 30 minutes, but longer is fine).

Bring the cream, milk and salt to the boil in a heavy-based saucepan with the cardamom, then leave for 15 minutes off the heat. Beat the eggs, egg yolk and sugar together. Pour the warm milk mixture on to this, stirring constantly.

Slice the brioche, butter it and layer it in a 2 litre (3½ pint) ovenproof dish, scattering the soaked cherries and any leftover pomegranate juice on as you layer the bread (try to get most of the cherries under the bread, or they might burn). Add some rose water to the egg and cream mixture – not too much – and a squeeze of lemon or lime juice, then taste it. You should be able to detect the rose water, but it shouldn't be too strong. Brands differ in strength, so you have to taste and decide if you need a little more.

Pour the egg and milk mixture evenly over the layers of bread. Leave the pudding to sit for 30 minutes; this will make it lighter.

Preheat the oven to 180°C fan (375°F), Gas Mark 5.

Put the dish into a roasting tin and carefully pour enough boiling water into the tin to come about one-third of the way up the sides of the dish. Bake for 40–45 minutes, or until puffy, golden and just set on the top. Remove the dish from the tin and leave to cool slightly – the pudding will continue to cook in the residual heat for a while – then dust with icing sugar before serving.

SERVES 6

6 just-ripe pears

100ml (3½fl oz) cassis

300ml (½ pint) red wine

60g (2¼oz) caster sugar

3 bay leaves

150g (5½oz) blackberries

CASSIS & BAY-BAKED PEARS WITH BLACKBERRIES

Pears are the most adaptable, well-behaved, rewarding fruits for autumn and winter puddings. Their flesh really sucks up other flavours, becoming imbued with red wine, Marsala, cinnamon, star anise or whatever else you choose. This is a 'very-beginning-of-autumn' dessert, to be made while blackberries are still around. Bay is underrated in sweet dishes; its peppery, slightly menthol flavour is subtle, but it provides a savoury hum. This is best made the day before serving, then the pears have time to take on the rich colour of the wine and cassis.

Preheat the oven to 180°C fan (375°F), Gas Mark 5.

Halve the pears – you don't need to peel or core them – and put them, cut sides up, into a gratin dish in which the fruit can sit quite snugly in a single layer. Pour the cassis and red wine over the pears, sprinkle with the sugar and tuck the bay leaves under the fruit.

Bake – spooning the juices over the pears from time to time – until the fruits are tender right through to the centre (how long this takes depends on the ripeness of the fruit; start checking after 20 minutes, but it could take as long as 35 minutes). It's a good idea to turn the pears over a couple of times while they're cooking.

By the time the fruit is cooked, the juice around it won't be thick, but should be syrupy and sweet enough to serve as it is. If you don't think it is, then remove the pears and bay leaves and reduce the juices by boiling them for a little while, leave to cool, then pour them back into the dish with the pears.

Add the berries about 30 minutes before you want to serve, spooning the juices over them, otherwise they get very soft sitting in the red wine syrup.

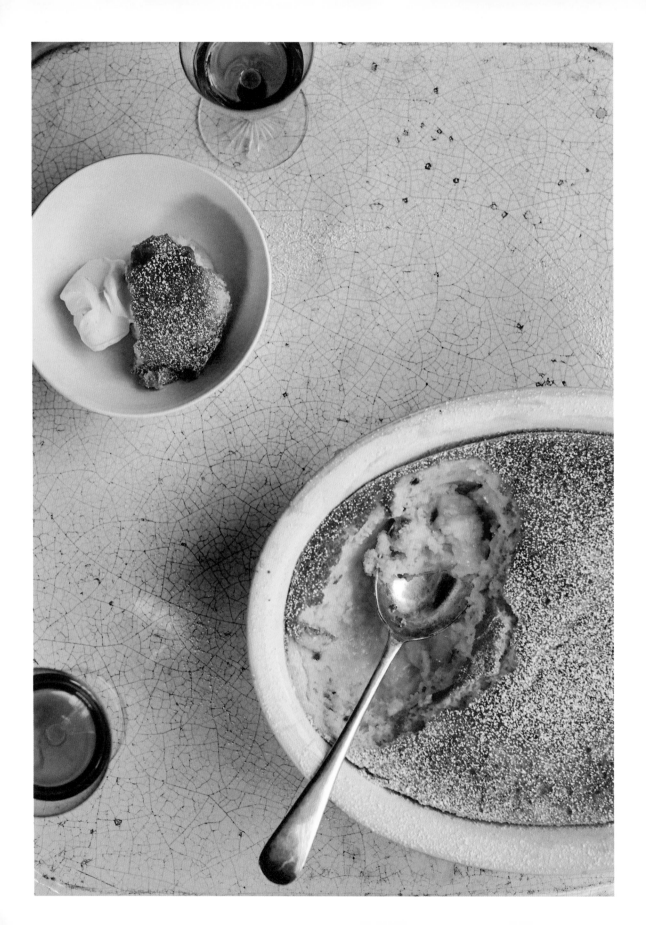

BAKED LIME, PASSION FRUIT & COCONUT PUDDING

SERVES 4–6

125g (4½oz) unsalted butter, at room temperature, plus more for the dish

200g (7oz) caster sugar

4 large eggs, separated

75g (2¾oz) self-raising flour

50g (1¾oz) desiccated coconut

400ml (14fl oz) whole milk

finely grated zest and juice of 3 limes

5 large, juicy passion fruits, or 6 smaller fruits

icing sugar, to serve

thick cream, to serve

A riff on the enduring and much-loved Australian classic, lemon delicious pudding. It's miraculous – a citrussy curd-cum-custard forms below the sponge as it cooks – and one of the simplest sweets you can have up your sleeve. A perfect Sunday lunch pudding.

Preheat the oven to 170°C fan (350°F), Gas Mark 4. Butter a 2 litre (3½ pint) ovenproof dish.

Throw the butter and sugar into a food processor and process until light and fluffy. Add the egg yolks and whizz the mixture, then add the flour and coconut, alternating with the milk, blending just until you have a smooth batter. Add the lime zest and juice, then scrape the batter into a large bowl.

Halve the passion fruits and scoop the pulp and seeds into a sieve placed over the bowl of batter. Push the pulp through the sieve into the batter, then add two-thirds of the black seeds, too (discard the remaining seeds).

Beat the egg whites until stiff. Using a large metal spoon, fold one-third of them into the batter to loosen it, then fold in the rest. Spoon into the prepared dish and set it in a roasting tin. Pour enough boiling water into the roasting tin to come halfway up the sides of the pudding dish and bake for 45 minutes.

Allow the pudding to cool a little when it comes out of the oven, then sift icing sugar over the top and serve with thick cream.

BAKED NECTARINES WITH PISTACHIOS & ROSE WATER

SERVES 6

6 nectarines, halved and pitted

100g (3½oz) shelled unsalted pistachio nuts

finely grated zest of ½ unwaxed lemon

1½ tablespoons caster sugar

1 small egg, lightly beaten

3 teaspoons rose water

300ml (½ pint) apple juice

icing sugar, to dust

nougat, to serve (optional)

cream, to serve

I prefer nectarines to the more usual peaches for this kind of dish, as their slight tartness contrasts well with the sweet filling. If you're not keen on rose water you can use orange flower water instead; I know they're both flower waters, but they give very different results. Serve the nectarines with little pieces of nougat, if you have some.

Preheat the oven to 180°C fan (375°F), Gas Mark 5.

Put the nectarine halves in a gratin dish in which they can lie in a single layer without too much space around them (otherwise the apple juice will reduce and burn).

Crush the pistachios roughly using a mortar and pestle, then mix in the lemon zest, sugar, egg and 1 teaspoon of the rose water. Fill the cavity of each nectarine with this stuffing, mounding it over the top if you have too much.

Mix the apple juice with the rest of the rose water and pour it around the nectarines. Bake for 30–45 minutes (the time it takes depends on the ripeness of the fruit). The nectarines should be tender and slightly caramelized on top.

Serve the fruit at room temperature, with a little icing sugar sifted on top and some of the cooking juices spooned around, and pieces of nougat, if you like. Cream never goes amiss, of course.

BAKED APPLES WITH TOASTED RYE, MINCEMEAT & CIDER BRANDY CREAM

SERVES 8

FOR THE APPLES AND
TOASTED RYE
15g (½oz) unsalted butter

80g (2¾oz) coarse rye or
pumpernickel breadcrumbs

35g (1¼oz) soft light
brown sugar

8 eating apples

225g (8oz) mincemeat

75g (2¾oz) dried cranberries

finely grated zest of
½ orange

15g (½oz) walnuts or
hazelnuts, roughly chopped

400ml (14fl oz) dry cider,
plus more if needed

FOR THE CREAM
300ml (½ pint) double or
whipping cream

2½ tablespoons soft light
brown sugar, or to taste

3 tablespoons cider brandy
or Calvados

This came about because I had to use up some mincemeat after Christmas; now I keep mincemeat just so I can make it. Eating apples make a much better dessert than unwieldy cookers, but don't use fruits that are too small, or you won't have room for the stuffing. I know they're an extra, but the breadcrumbs really do make this.

Preheat the oven to 180°C fan (375°F), Gas Mark 5.

For the rye crumbs, melt the butter in a frying pan, then cook until it starts to brown a little. Remove from the heat and stir in the breadcrumbs and sugar. Spread this out on a baking sheet (it's important that the mixture is not in clumps) and bake for 20 minutes, tossing a few times during baking, until toasted. Leave to cool.

Slice the top off each apple to make a lid about 5cm (2in) across, then core each one. Remove a little of the flesh around the core, too (use it for a smoothie or something).

Put the apples in an ovenproof dish or roasting tin in which they can sit close to each other; you don't want masses of space around them.

Mix the mincemeat with the cranberries, orange zest and nuts and spoon this into each apple, sprinkling any leftovers into the dish, then put the apple lids on. Pour the cider around the apples.

Bake for 30–40 minutes, or until the apples are completely tender, spooning the juices up over them every so often. Do keep an eye on the apples, as they can go from tender to burst and falling apart very suddenly.

Whip the cream until it's holding its shape, then whisk in the brown sugar and cider brandy or Calvados. Serve the apples with their juices, adding a dollop of cider brandy cream and a scattering of the rye crumbs.

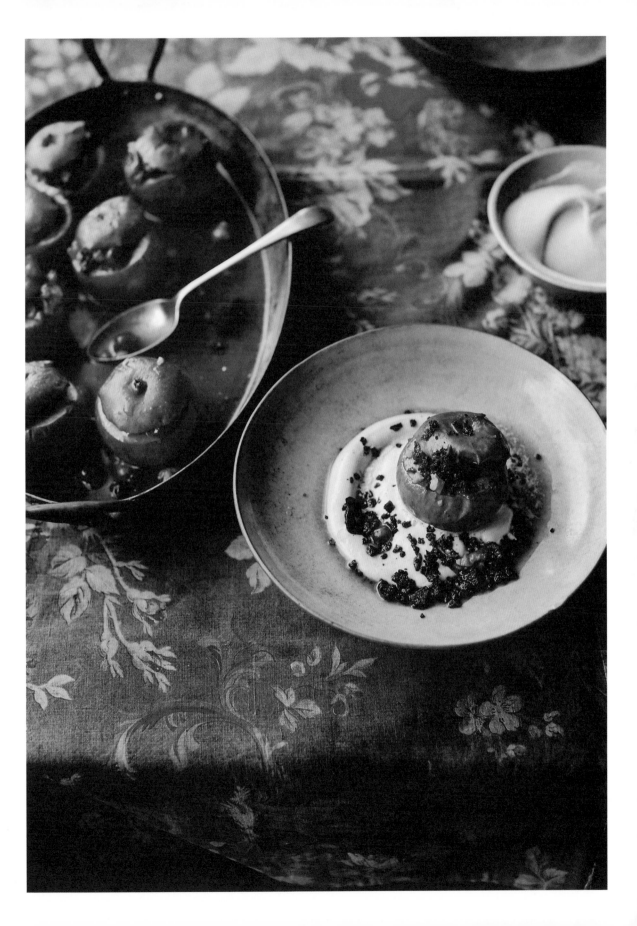

SHOPPING

Nearly every ingredient can be bought online nowadays, though I've tried, throughout this book, to suggest alternatives for harder-to-source foods. I don't imagine there is a single food you can't find from the companies below. You probably have your own local butcher or favourite fishmonger, but I've listed some great online butchers (my own favourite butcher is two bus rides away so I often shop online for meat). We all depend on supermarkets, but even the best are not good for pork – I'd definitely buy that at a good butcher – or mackerel (it's never fresh enough). When buying dry goods, it's best to make a long list of ingredients and get them from one source (Souschef has nearly everything), as that way you save on delivery costs.

FARMISON & CO

www.farmison.com

An excellent online butcher. I use them all the time.

HEALTHY SUPPLIES

www.healthysupplies.co.uk

Not just for 'healthy' ingredients, this company has lots of different foods, but is a particularly great source for pulses, wholegrains, seeds, nuts and dried fruits.

MELBURY AND APPLETON

www.melburyandappleton.co.uk

Another very good website, where ingredients are listed by country. Also great for grains and pulses.

PIPERS FARM

www.pipersfarm.com

An award-winning Devon-based company that I have used over the years for meat. Their sausages aren't made with nitrates or nitrites, the preserving chemicals used in salamis and most sausages that have been linked with cancer. This means their sausages have a short shelf life, so they send them out frozen. You can then store them in the freezer, or defrost them and cook them quickly.

SEASONED PIONEERS

www.seasonedpioneers.co.uk

This is where I often go for unusual spices. I've been using them for years.

SOUSCHEF

www.souschef.co.uk

Don't be put off by the name. They don't just cater for chefs. There's not much you can't find on this site.

THE ASIAN COOKSHOP

www.theasiancookshop.co.uk

A vast array of foods, including every pulse you've ever heard of (and some you haven't). They have specialist ingredients for Burmese, Caribbean, Chinese, Indian, Japanese, Mexican and Thai food.

THE COOL CHILE COMPANY

www.coolchile.co.uk

The best stockist for unusual dried chillies, especially South American varieties.

TURNER & GEORGE

www.turnerandgeorge.co.uk

Another favourite butcher – they have a shop in London as well – with really well-sourced meat and poultry.

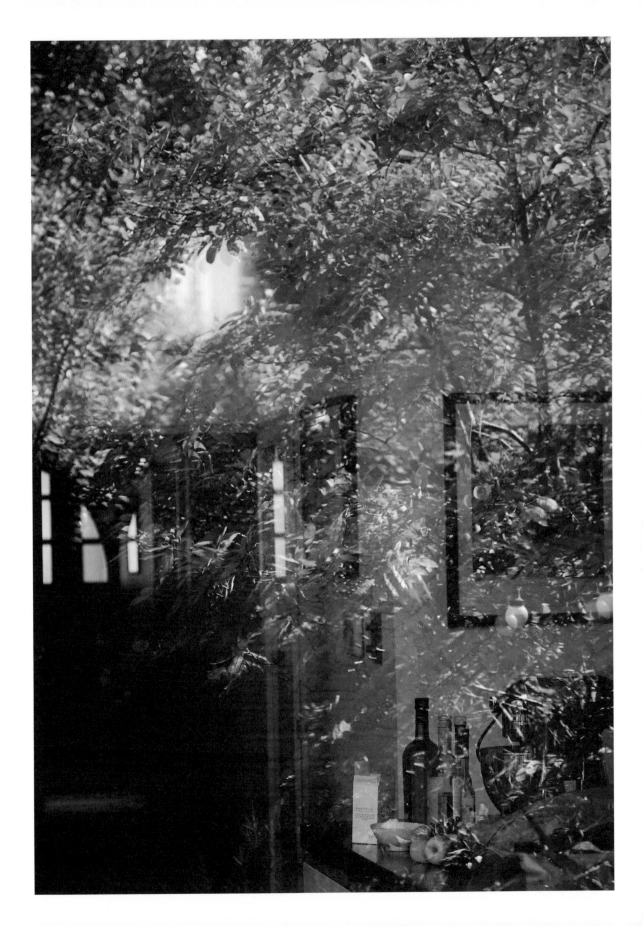

An Hachette UK Company
www.hachette.co.uk

First published in Great Britain in 2019 by Mitchell Beazley,
a division of Octopus Publishing Group Ltd
Carmelite House
50 Victoria Embankment
London EC4Y 0DZ
www.octopusbooks.co.uk

Text copyright © Diana Henry 2019
Design and layout copyright © Octopus Publishing Group 2019
Photography copyright © Laura Edwards 2019

ISBN 978 1 78472 584 6

A CIP catalogue record for this book is available
from the British Library.

Printed and bound in China

10 9 8 7 6 5 4 3 2 1

Group Publishing Director: Denise Bates
Creative Director: Jonathan Christie
Photographer: Laura Edwards
Photographic assistant: Sam Harris
Design and Art Direction: Miranda Harvey
Editor: Lucy Bannell
Home Economist and Food Stylist: Joss Herd
Assistant Home Economist: India Whiley-Morton
Senior Production Manager: Katherine Hockley

The recipes in this book were all tested in Diana Henry's oven
on the fan setting, which – on her oven – equates to about 10°C
(50°F) less than a conventional oven. All the conversions to
Fahrenheit and Gas Mark were driven by this. Your oven may
differ; we recommend you check it with an oven thermometer.

For Amy Bryant, with love and thanks

ACKNOWLEDGEMENTS

Huge thanks, yet again, to my team – Laura Edwards, Miranda Harvey, Lucy Bannell and Joss Herd – for their perfectionism and tremendously hard work. Also to our assistant food stylist, India Whiley-Morton, and photographer's assistant Sam Harris. Never have so many roasting tins been washed by so few people for just one book. (And thank you, Sam, for displaying the best priorities by starting to organize the shoot lunch from 11am every day. You're the man.)

Extra thanks to Lucy Bannell on this title as she didn't just edit it but also tested some of the recipes. In the last stages – when I had a very ill child – I don't know what I would have done without you, Lucy.

Thanks also to the team at Octopus, my publisher Denise Bates, creative director Jonathan Christie, and Frances Johnson and Katherine Hockley in production.

My friend and fellow food writer Melissa Clark generously gave me her recipe for butterflied lamb with yogurt and herb sauce on page 193, (Melissa writes for *The New York Times* and you'll find her eminently cookable recipes on their website). Thanks also to Von Diaz for allowing me to use a slightly amended version of her wonderful dish, sweet and sour chicken and chorizo in adobo, from her book *Coconuts and Collards* (University Press of Florida). Chef Andrew Clarke from St Leonard's restaurant in London helped me to create a home cook-friendly version of his roast cabbage with XO crumbs. It's one of the best dishes on his menu, so this is especially generous.

I have spent decades picking up ceramics in a very ad hoc way, but for this book I actually tracked down some wonderful additions. Thank you to Jono Smart and Emily Stephen, and to Pottery West for knowing just what I needed and for their generosity. Netherton Foundry, makers of superb pans, your kindness knows no bounds. Thank you for pans, baking sheets, skillets, and for driving from Shropshire when it was needed.

All cookbooks depend on good suppliers. The food stylists and I would like to give a huge shout-out to Kent & Son's Butchers of St John's Wood and Humphrey's Butchers in Saffron Walden for getting us great meat, often at short notice.

Finally, a massive thanks to Amy Bryant, my editor at *The Sunday Telegraph,* to whom this book is dedicated, for years of sifting through ideas, spotting mistakes in recipes and endless support, friendship and kindness.